Dear Reader,

I want to share with you simple principles and ideas that will help you experience abundant fruit for God's kingdom. It may not be an accident that this book is in your hands. The Lord may be calling you to experience more fruit for His kingdom – more fruit than you have ever imagined.

Ordinary believers are having an extraordinary impact for God's kingdom and are seeing God move through them in powerful ways. Whether you are an outgoing person or shy person, you are about to discover people like you who are having an extraordinary impact.

I pray that this book will help unleash you to touch even more lives than you've ever imagined – for the sake of the Gospel.

Jesus said that he came to bind up the brokenhearted. There are so many people in our world who are broken and desperately need to hear the Gospel.

Even if you feel ordinary, you may be able to reach many people for Christ. Will you join me in this journey into greater fruitfulness? … I hope so!

In Christ,
R. N. Berguson

This book is dedicated to my father, Johnny Berguson. For over a decade, my father traveled as an evangelist, sharing God's love with thousands of people. Without his love for people and his commitment to helping people find life-transforming faith in Christ, I would not have been inspired to write this book. Dad, thanks for your inspiration and for being such a role model in showing me what it means to love people in the name of Christ.

BEFORE YOU READ THIS BOOK...

Before you begin the 40 days, you can visit www.40DaysToFruitfulness.com. At this website, you'll hear about other people whose lives have been transformed to greater fruitfulness through this book. You'll also be able to track your own progress as you journey into greater fruitfulness.

If you visit the site *before* reading this book, you will find helpful tools for your 40-day journey into greater fruitfulness. You can also subscribe to a podcast or emails to encourage you along your journey. I'm excited about what God is going to do through you! ॐ

The Vine and the Branches (John 15)

"I am the true vine, and my Father is the gardener. He cuts off every branch in me that bears no fruit, while every branch that does bear fruit he prunes so that it will be even more fruitful. You are already clean because of the word I have spoken to you. Remain in me, and I will remain in you. No branch can bear fruit by itself; it must remain in the vine. Neither can you bear fruit unless you remain in me.

I am the vine; you are the branches. If a man remains in me and I in him, he will bear much fruit; apart from me you can do nothing. If anyone does not remain in me, he is like a branch that is thrown away and withers; such branches are picked up, thrown into the fire and burned. If you remain in me and my words remain in you, ask whatever you wish, and it will be given you. This is to my Father's glory, that you bear much fruit, showing yourselves to be my disciples.

As the Father has loved me, so have I loved you. Now remain in my love. If you obey my commands, you will remain in my love, just as I have obeyed my Father's commands and remain in his love. I have told you this so that my joy may be in you and that your joy may be complete. My command is this: Love each other as I have loved you. Greater love has no one than this, that he lay down his life for his friends. You are my friends if you do what I command.

I no longer call you servants, because a servant does not know his master's business. Instead, I have called you friends, for everything that I learned from my Father I have made known to you. You did not choose me, but <u>I chose you and appointed you to go and bear fruit—fruit that will last.</u> Then the Father will give you whatever you ask in my name. This is my command: Love each other."

– John 15:1-17 (NIV, emphasis added)

Day #1 – Getting Started, Part I

My father, Johnny Berguson, was a traveling evangelist for over a decade. I remember traveling with my entire family around the country for many years. During this time, we saw thousands and thousands of people make commitments to Christ.

Our family would put on a horse show with a specially-trained, Arabian horse. The horse, known as Sheik, was trained to perform many tricks such as fetching like a dog and backing through mazes. Then, my father would present the Gospel at the end of the horse show.

This was my life from just after I was born until my teenage years. Growing up, I became used to people *hearing* the Gospel <u>and</u> *responding* to the Gospel. Many churches and Christians are not used to people *hearing* and *responding* to the Gospel on a regular basis. It is my prayer that as you apply the principles in this book *you too* will become used to people *hearing* and *responding* to the Gospel as a normal and exciting part of life.

Oftentimes, people tend to think that there needs to be a *"dramatic"* move of God for anyone to be saved. In the book of Acts, it talks about people being added to the church *daily*! There were dramatic moves of God in Acts, but people were also reached during daily life.

When a farmer plants seeds, the farmer expects a harvest. The farmer may not receive a sevenfold, mega harvest from everything planted but the farmer always expects a crop. Unfortunately, many Christians and churches plant seeds hoping that "some year" there will be something that comes up from the ground. Just imagine if farmers did this!

Or, imagine the news announcing… *"Farmer Brown planted seeds this year. Miraculously, he had a harvest and plants are coming up! Farmers everywhere are flocking to see the plants growing on Farmer Brown's farm. Folks, this is incredible. Farmer Brown did not know if anything would happen when he planted the seeds. Not every seed reaped a harvest, but he definitely had a harvest. Farmer Brown is now wondering if he keeps planting seeds if new plants will keep coming up."*

Just like a farmer anticipates a harvest when seeds are planted, individual believers and congregations should also anticipate a harvest from planting seeds. Not every week will be like an Acts chapter 2 harvest where three thousand people were added to the church in one day (you may never see a week like Acts chapter 2!). However, your life should bear at least some fruit on an ongoing basis. Jesus said that we should bear fruit (John 15).

At the same time, it is important to realize that some believers are better at planting and some are better at harvesting. Regardless of the role, every Christian has been commanded to share the good news of the Gospel with unbelievers

(Matthew 28:18-20). The lost desperately need to hear the message of the Gospel.

Power Thought for Today

The Bible consistently uses farming and fishing analogies to describe how people come to Christ. Make a commitment to approach witnessing as a farmer or fisher of men.

"As Jesus was walking beside the Sea of Galilee, he saw two brothers, Simon called Peter and his brother Andrew. They were casting a net into the lake, for they were fishermen. 'Come, follow me,' Jesus said, 'and I will make you fishers of men.' At once they left their nets and followed him."
                                                        – Matthew 4:18-20 (NIV)

Application

As you begin your journey into greater fruitfulness, identify thoughts and beliefs that have held you back in sharing your faith. Ask the Lord to change your thoughts and beliefs to align with His Word. Pray that the Lord would give you the heart and desire to make outreach and the Great Commission a part of your daily lifestyle. Pray that the Lord would begin to open your eyes to see people each day who need to hear the Gospel. May the Lord transform you into a fisher of men.

Daily Journal

What are thoughts and beliefs that have held you back in sharing your faith?

_____

_____

_____

_____

_____

What opportunities have you had recently to share your faith?

_____

_____

_____

_____

Please write your prayer for today and ask God to help you learn how to share your faith more effectively…

_____

_____

_____

_____

Day #2 – Getting Started, Part II

There is a longing within each of us to have an impact that lasts. Some of the greatest moments in my life have been when someone repents of their sins and gives their heart and life to Jesus. It is a time for rejoicing when someone repents and turns to Christ. In the Scriptures, it says that when one sinner repents the angels in heaven rejoice!

May you have some God-appointed moments over the next 40 days where you see someone's life changed for eternity. Pray that the Lord will grow your desire for outreach during these 40 days of fruitfulness.

Power Thought for Today

Too often we want to share our faith, but we wait. We wait for another day, a better opportunity, or more boldness. Sometimes, we even wait for someone else to reach out to the person we know.

"My food," said Jesus, "is to do the will of him who sent me and to finish his work. Do you not say, 'Four months more and then the harvest'? I tell you, open your eyes and look at the fields! They are ripe for harvest. Even now the reaper draws his wages, even now he harvests the crop for eternal life, so that the sower and the reaper may be glad together.

– John 4: 34 (NIV)

One CD opens the door to a conversation about church

Two friends went to a donut shop one Sunday night. The one friend gave the young lady behind the counter a sermon CD from that day's church service, explaining that it was a gift for her. Beth, the lady behind the counter, was very thankful for the gift and expressed her appreciation.

When the two friends sat down, Beth asked the two friends where the church met. The two ladies soon got into a short conversation with Beth. They learned that she and her husband had just moved to the area three months ago. She did not have any friends in the area, and she had an interest in church. The two ladies invited Beth and her husband to a church event.

As the two friends left the donut shop, they knew they had just made a divine connection. They had just prayed that the Lord would give them opportunities to reach out with the Gospel that very same day at church. And, it was so easy and natural. One small CD opened the door to an important conversation!

Dog leads to outreach opportunity

A while back, my father (Johnny) was traveling and had taken his dogs with him on the trip. One afternoon, he decided to take his dogs to Dog Park. He was not expecting to meet anyone at Dog Park. He just thought that there would be a lot of dogs at the park. While at Dog Park, he met another man walking his dog. They got into a conversation, and the conversation quickly turned to spiritual things.

The man said that he wished he could know for sure that he was going to heaven. My father briefly shared the Gospel with the man. Unfortunately, he only had about two minutes to share the Gospel. He wished he had a CD with him to give to the man so he would be able to hear even more about the Gospel. This was a reminder to my father that he needed to keep messages with him at all times. It is important to be prepared – you never know when you might have an opportunity to share the Gospel with someone. ⟡

Application

As you begin your journey into greater outreach and fruitfulness, select several outreach and sermon messages that you can begin carrying with you wherever you go. Women can carry messages in their purse while men can take messages in their briefcase, a backpack, or car. Choose messages that you would enjoy giving away to people that you meet as you go through daily life. Don't wait another day – begin carrying messages and resources with you today!

Daily Journal

What are some messages and materials that you are going to carry with you? Where and when will you get these materials?

_____

_____

_____

What opportunities have you had recently to share your faith?

_____

_____

_____

_____

_____

Please write your prayer for today. Ask God to give you opportunities today and in the future to share the Gospel with those who need to hear the good news.

_____

_____

_____

_____

_____

Day #3 – Hope for the Depressed and Suicidal

There are many hurting and oppressed people in nearly every community. Some people have been deeply wounded by a parent, friend, relative, or someone they know. Others have been oppressed by addictions, and still others are lacking meaning and fulfillment in life.

Depression and despair are becoming rampant as people put their trust and hope in things other than Christ. When you encounter the broken and hurting, you have an opportunity to reach out to them by sharing the hope of the Gospel. Jesus sets people free and breaks the chains of their oppression!

May the Lord give you eyes to see when people are hurting and help you reach out to them with the message of the good news of the Gospel. Reaching out to hurting people is something close to Christ's heart. Over and over again in the Gospels, Jesus reaches out to those in pain.

"The LORD is close to the brokenhearted and saves those who are crushed in spirit." — Psalm 34:18 (NIV)

Power Thought for Today

In Jesus' day, there were many hurting and brokenhearted people. According to the Scriptures, Jesus was sent to heal the brokenhearted and set captive people free. There are so many hurting people who need to hear the good news of the Gospel in our world today. May the Lord equip you to share with those in need.

> *"The Spirit of the LORD is upon Me,*
> *Because He has anointed Me*
> *To preach the Gospel to the poor;*
> *He has sent Me to heal the brokenhearted,*
> *To proclaim liberty to the captives*
> *And recovery of sight to the blind,*
> *To set at liberty those who are oppressed;*
> *To proclaim the acceptable year of the LORD."*
> — Luke 4:18-19 (NKJV, emphasis added)

Woman rescued from suicide!

Marion was temporarily living in England, but her life was one of despair. For months, day and night, she couldn't sleep. She was on antidepressants because she couldn't stop crying and worrying. Marion couldn't handle it anymore; she didn't want to live. She would sit in a dark room and think of ways to not go on. This all changed though!

One day, she received a phone call from Kathy, a friend of hers in the United States. Kathy could tell that Marion was not doing well. She desperately wanted to encourage her because she knew Marion was alone. The only economical way that Kathy knew to do this was to send encouraging messages of her pastor's sermons. So, she boxed up several messages and sent them to England. She called Marion a week later to see if she had received the messages and if she had listened to them. But, she didn't have to ask. Kathy could simply tell by Marion's voice that the messages had impacted Marion. Marion then told her that she had been listening to the recordings over and over again.

Soon, Marion began to pray, read the Bible, and listen to even more sermons of Kathy's pastor. Marion found a hope that saved her life through these messages. Marion's life changed dramatically as she found faith in Christ and a reason worth living.

Messages help depressed and suicidal family member just in time!

One lady sent copies of her pastor's sermons to her sister-in-law who was depressed and contemplating suicide. The sister-in-law started looking forward to receiving the messages, because they often addressed the issues that concerned her. The lady was thrilled that the messages touched her sister-in-law's heart so deeply. Her sister-in-law felt God's love through the recorded messages, and God used these messages to lead her back to church.

27 year old man saved after a life of smoking, drinking, and gambling!

A life of smoking, drinking, and gambling left a 27 year old man in financial ruin and in a very broken relationship with his parents. He was in such a hopeless state that he seriously considered taking his own life. But all that changed when he was given a recording with a Biblical message on it. Through the message, he felt God's love urging him not to destroy himself, but to receive eternal life. This young man repented of all his bad habits and started to follow Jesus. Now he prays, reads his Bible daily, and attends church regularly. He is a new person with hope, peace, and a new reason to live. He is very grateful for the recorded message that led him to these blessings and his new life in Christ. ॐ

Application

In each of these stories, someone cared enough to share a message of hope with the lost and hurting. Pray that the Lord will lead you to people who need to hear the Gospel. Pray that He would give you wisdom in reaching out to people in need of hope.

Daily Journal

Who are some people you know that are hurting and really need to hear the good news of the Gospel? How do you believe God wants you to reach out to them?

_____

_____

_____

What opportunities have you had recently to share your faith?

_____

_____

_____

_____

Please write your prayer for today. Ask God to give you opportunities to reach out to the hurting and broken. (Tip: Make sure you carry messages of hope that you can share with the hurting and broken.)

_____

_____

_____

_____

_____

Day #4 - Family, Part I

hen witnessing to family members, it often takes a lot of perseverance. As you wait for God to touch the hearts of your family, be patient with your family members and persistent in prayer.

It is important to live out your faith in words and deeds. As family members see God at work in your life and your complete trust in Him, it will create even more opportunities to share with them about Christ. These opportunities may not always occur right away, but you can pray and persevere until they come. You may see surprising and unexpected opportunities open up for you to share the Gospel with your family!

Power Thought for Today

When we come to know Jesus, it is natural to want our family members to find Christ as well. Sometimes, family members come to Christ quickly and other times, it becomes a long journey. We need to commit ourselves to the journey, long or short.

God may use your witness to family members not only to reach them but to build patience and persistence in your own life.

"He then brought them out and asked, 'Sirs, what must I do to be saved?' They replied, 'Believe in the Lord Jesus, and you will be saved— you and your household.' Then they spoke the word of the Lord to him and to all the others in his house. At that hour of the night the jailer took them and washed their wounds; then immediately he and all his family were baptized." – Acts 16:30-33 (NIV)

A young child helps lead her father to Christ!

A young child really wanted her father to come to Christ, but he lived in another state. She realized that she could use messages and the post office to help share with her father the good news of the Gospel. This young girl started sending her father copies of her pastor's sermons. Before too long, her father decided to put his faith in Jesus. This man's life was forever changed, because his young daughter cared enough to reach out to him! Even children can help people, even family members, to find faith in Christ!

CD helps brother come to Christ!

The first time that one young lady took a CD for evangelistic purposes, she had no idea that it would be the tool God would use to rescue her brother's life. She had witnessed to her brother a few days before, but the conversation had ended in an argument. Despite her brother's resistance, she knew he needed to hear the Gospel. The young lady was in the car driving her brother to college when she decided to play the CD. She could tell God was using it, because her brother was listening carefully. At the conclusion of the message, she asked him if he wanted to pray to receive Christ, and he agreed.

Fifteen months later the young lady says that her brother is "doing awesome, growing by leaps and bounds, going to church, and soaking up the Word of God." He has already started serving the Lord by translating the very message that God used to save him into the French language, so that many more can hear about how salvation can be found in Jesus Christ!

Brother saved through persistence

For 12 years, Randall sent tapes to his brother who was in the Army and was not walking with the Lord. Every month or two, Randall would select a sermon tape or music and mail it from his home in Kentucky to wherever his brother was stationed in the world at the time. "He kept telling me he listened to them," says Randall. "He also said they drove him crazy because he knew he needed to get right with God, but he was putting it off." After 12 persistent and prayerful years, Randall's brother turned to Christ. Randall's brother still listens to messages in order to strengthen his faith! ✺

Application

In these stories, people came to faith in Christ as their family members were faithful to share messages. In two of the three stories where family members were reached, messages were shared more than once. In one of the stories above, it took 12 years to reach one family member? Are you ready to be that persistent? Pray that the Lord would give you persistence and wisdom in reaching out to your family members.

Daily Journal

Which of your family members need your prayers for their salvation?

_____

_____

_____

What opportunities have you had recently to share your faith?

_____

_____

_____

_____

Please write your prayer for today. Ask God to give you wisdom and persistence in reaching your family members. Ask the Lord which family members you should begin sharing messages with.

_____

_____

_____

_____

_____

Day #5 - Family, Part II

n reaching family members, it takes not only sharing the Gospel with them, but oftentimes, your family members need to see the impact of the Gospel in your life as well.

As the Gospel impacts your life, your family members will see the impact in your life. At other times, when one family member makes a commitment to Christ, other family members will soon make a commitment to Christ.

Family members do not always come to Christ immediately. If it takes a long time for your family members to come to Christ, be encouraged by the story of the persistent widow (see Luke 18). Jesus told us this story so that we would be persistent in prayer and not give up.

Power Thought for Today

When you come to Christ, your life can become a light to those around you including your family. The Lord wants your light – the light of Christ reigning in your life – to shine so that people will see your actions and give glory to God. The light from your life may impact your family and those you meet for eternity.

"You are the light of the world. A city on a hill cannot be hidden. Neither do people light a lamp and put it under a bowl. Instead they put it on its stand, and it gives light to everyone in the house. In the same way, let your light shine before men, that they may see your good deeds and praise your Father in heaven."
— Matthew 5:14-16 (NIV, emphasis added)

Whole family gets saved!

Some people see their families come to Christ as they share timely messages that family members need to hear. A Georgia woman was saved through a recorded message she received. She then shared messages with her whole family – they were saved as well! Now, they all carry messages to pass along to others that they meet.

A family member shares a message that leads an airline pilot to church!

An airline pilot started attending church because a family member gave him recorded messages. After attending church for a month, he invited the pastor to fly with him. They flew to a small city and had lunch together. As they were walking back to the plane, the pastor asked the pilot if he was ready to give his heart to Christ. The pilot knelt down under the wing of the plane and gave his life to Jesus. Now this pilot uses his influence for the kingdom of God. This impact resulted from one family member who cared enough to give him recorded messages. Messages can be used to share the Gospel with even hard to reach family members, like an airplane pilot.

Desperate man receives sermon messages from his sister!

One desperate man, who had lost his family, regularly received sermon messages from his sister. "One Sunday on a construction site," said the pastor of Gospel Lighthouse Church, "he listened to a message about Abraham's men and gave his heart back to God. Now he is one of the key leaders in the church, a fired up man – and every week, he takes (recorded messages) and gives them to people!"

Application

Pray and ask the Lord to help your light shine to your family members and others. Ask the Lord to give you opportunities to reach out to your family members. Perhaps the Lord will give you an opportunity to share a sermon CD, a testimony, or other special message with a family member.

If you have family members that live far away, you can send these family members messages. Many family members have been saved as people cared enough to send them messages.

One good idea is to write down the names of your family members on an index card and pray for them everyday. Pray that the Lord would bless your family and help your unsaved family members find new life in Christ.

Daily Journal

Which family members are on your heart to pray for their salvation? What messages and materials could you start sharing with your family members?

_____

_____

_____

Have you had any opportunities recently to share your faith with your family members?

_____

_____

_____

Please write your prayer for today. Ask the Lord to help your light shine to your family members and others.

_____

_____

_____

_____

_____

Day #6 – Seeing God Move At Work

cross the world, there is a growing awareness of God moving in the workplace. Even in corporate America, there seems to be a crying out for values and principles after the scandals in recent years. Spiritual hunger is increasing as more and more people seek deeper meaning in life. It would not be surprising if revival starts happening in our workplaces before too long.

Pray that the Lord will use you to reach those around you and give you opportunities to share the Gospel.

Power Thought for Today

Wherever people gather is where the Gospel needs to go. The marketplace is a prime place where people gather.

In the New Testament, Jesus and his disciples took the Gospel into the marketplace. The Lord may use you to take the Gospel into the marketplace.

The Scripture describes Paul while he was in Athens as sharing with people *daily* in the marketplace.

"So he (Paul) reasoned in the synagogue with the Jews and the God-fearing Greeks, as well as in the <u>marketplace</u> day by day with those who happened to be there." — Acts 17:17 (NIV, emphasis added)

Plant managers impacted by a persistent lady and a sermon message!

One lady wanted to start a Bible study and prayer meeting in the manufacturing plant where she worked. The managers kept turning her down, saying, "No, no, this isn't the place for that." Then she decided to take another approach. She took a copy of one of her pastor's messages and gave it not only to her supervisor but to the plant manager as well. Now that took a lot of guts, especially after she had been turned down repeatedly for these Bible studies and prayer meetings. The very next week she was called into the office.

Guess what they said?

The plant manager told her, "We were really moved by that message." It was incredible! That was the start of a weekly Bible study meeting at that plant.

Man gives his co-workers messages as Christmas gifts…

A man felt inspired to give his coworkers nicely packaged messages as Christmas gifts. One of the co-workers who received a message as a gift was a man named Eric. The message impacted Eric greatly. For the next several months, Eric asked for more messages on a weekly basis. Finally, Eric went to church to meet the pastor and to tell him that the recordings had changed his life. His life had been filled with anger, drugs, violence, and imprisonment. Eric made a commitment to Christ and made Jesus the Lord of his life. His life was changed completely, and he started serving others.

This man helped his boss find Christ!

A young man in Virginia found his work environment challenging. He wished that he did not have to hear the vulgar language at his workplace on a regular basis. This young man was willing to take a step of faith. He gave his boss a CD of a sermon from his church. Eventually, he was able to discuss the message with his boss. As a result, his boss came to Christ!

One message travels through seven floors of an office building!

Another person took a copy of a message with them to work. This person shared the recorded message with a friend and said, "This is one of the most meaningful messages I've ever heard." That friend then told another coworker, and that coworker shared the message with another coworker. And the cycle kept repeating. That one recorded message traveled through seven floors of their office building as it was passed from person to person. Just imagine if you shared a CD that was passed through an entire company. ฿

Application

Using CDs and recorded messages can be an easy way to share your faith with coworkers. You may not have time to have a lengthy discussion about the Gospel in the workplace, but you do have time to share a message with someone in need. Another way that people are sharing the Gospel at work is by having a fishbowl or some type of container on their desk that is filled with messages and has a little sign that says "FREE, Take one!" Pray that the Lord will give you wisdom in sharing the Gospel in the workplace, and that the Lord will cause people to cross your path at strategic times.

Here are several ideas that people are using at work to reach their coworkers for Christ:

1. Pray for the Lord to connect you with people at work each day who could benefit from hearing the messages that you have. Keep several messages with you at the office.
2. Put out a fishbowl containing FREE CDs on your desk.
3. Keep a supply of messages on important topics that your coworkers may be facing or addressing in their lives. Having more messages gives you more opportunities for outreach.
4. Start a weekly lunchtime small group on "Exploring the Bible" or "Exploring Faith." Invite people to this group. You may be amazed at how many pre-Christians are willing to join an "Exploring" Bible study. Give people who attend this small group recorded messages from time to time.
5. Pray, pray, pray! Then, do what God speaks to your heart.

Daily Journal

What are some ways that you could reach those in the workplace or through your profession?

_____

_____

_____

What opportunities have you had recently to share your faith?

_____

_____

_____

_____

Please write your prayer for today. Pray that the Lord would connect you with people at work who need to hear the Gospel. Ask God for wisdom in implementing ideas to reach people at work or in business.

_____

_____

_____

_____

_____

Day #7 – Friends, Part I

Sharing Christ with friends is a very common form of outreach and evangelism. Countless lives have been touched as friends have shared with friends about Christ. Since you genuinely care about your friends, it is very natural to desire to share the good news of what Christ has done in your life with your friends.

Ask the Lord to give you opportunities to share Christ with your friends. Be vigilant in praying for the salvation of your friends.

Power Thought for Today

Friends have an influence on friends. The best influence you can have on your friends is to help them find the Light of the Savior, Jesus Christ. Pray that the Lord will help you to be prepared to share the Gospel with your friends. Or, perhaps, you will have the right recorded message at the right time to share with your friends.

"But in your hearts set apart Christ as Lord. Always be prepared to give an answer to everyone who asks you to give the reason for the hope that you have. But do this with gentleness and respect..."

– I Peter 3:15 (NIV)

Man listens to sermons in his basement and gets saved!

Bruce's salvation happened during a time in his life when he really wasn't serving the Lord – lip service maybe, but not real commitment.

A Christian friend of Bruce's volunteered to help him build a recreation room in his basement. When he showed up at Bruce's door, he had a hammer, a saw, and a portable stereo player. He asked Bruce if it was OK if he listened to some sermon messages from his church while they worked. When his friend left that night, he told Bruce that he would leave the player and teaching messages so that they could listen to them the next night. Well, his friend was unable to come the next evening, but Bruce continued listening to the messages by himself.

To make a long story short, about three or four nights later, Bruce asked Jesus to be his Lord and Savior right there in his basement. And, it was all because someone cared enough about him to lend him some messages and a stereo. You never know when you might share a few CDs with someone that may change their life for eternity.

Teenage girl helps lead a friend to Christ!

A teenage girl noticed the lost state of her friend. This teenager cared enough about her friend to give her friend a recorded Biblical message. God used that message to create a hunger for the Lord in her friend's life. The very next Sunday, the friend came to church and gave her life to Jesus Christ.

Application

In these stories, friends cared enough about friends to share the Gospel with them. Some people make praying for their friends and the salvation of unsaved friends a daily part of their prayer time each day. By writing down the names of each of your friends, it makes it easy to remember to pray for them each day.

You may have a friend on your heart right now that you are concerned about the state of their soul. Pray and ask the Lord to give you opportunities to share the Gospel with your friends. Just like the people in today's stories, you may be able to give CD messages, testimonies, or other recorded messages to your friends that impact their lives for eternity.

Daily Journal

Write down the names of friends that you will pray the Lord brings into the kingdom of God. Pray for their salvation daily.

_____

_____

_____

_____

What opportunities have you had recently to share your faith?

_____

_____

_____

_____

Please write your prayer for today. Pray for opportunities to share messages and the good news of the Gospel with your friends.

_____

_____

_____

_____

Day #8 –Friends, Part II

Friends interact with each other at all different types of locations. Wherever people gather is where friends make connections with friends.

People also make new friends as they connect with new people at places they visit frequently. It could be the daycare, the hair salon, the workplace, the chiropractor, the grocery store, or the favorite gas station. Just think through all the different places where you have met new friends. Connections with others and friendships may form just about anywhere.

You probably have some friends on your heart that you are hoping and praying for their salvation. It does not have to be difficult to share Christ with your friends.

Power Thought for Today

Each of us has friends who need to hear the good news of the Gospel. You may be the only person who ever shares the Gospel with your friends. Your friends may not hear the Gospel unless you tell them. This is a big responsibility. Jesus laid down his life for us. This should inspire us to give of our lives to others. You can lay down your life for your unsaved friends by consistently praying for them, serving them, and sharing your hope in Christ with them.

I have heard countless stories of friends helping friends find Christ as they gave them a sermon CD or other recorded message. I wouldn't be a very good friend if I did not share the most important thing in my life - my faith - with my friends. If I kept my faith that has transformed my life a secret, I would not be a true friend! I want my friends to find hope in Christ, and I am sure you do too.

"My command is this: Love each other as I have loved you. Greater love has no one than this, that he lay down his life for his friends."
– John 15:12-13 (NIV)

CD given by a friend helps a mother find Christ!

On a typical day, Casi takes her daughter to preschool and heads off to work. This is perfectly normal, like thousands of mothers. During this daily routine, Casi met Rachelle. "Rachelle told me she went to Victory Church," shared Casi. "She wasn't pushy, just compassionate. She told me she wanted me to hear Pastor Josh. She gave me several CDs containing sermons of Pastor Josh."

"I was hesitant to listen to the sermons," admits Casi, "and Rachelle would ask regularly if I had listened to them yet. Eventually, I decided that I should at least humor her and listen."

As Casi listened to the messages, she felt the life-changing power of the message of Jesus Christ. "I couldn't believe my ears," exclaimed Casi. "Pastor Josh was talking to me. What he was saying related to my life. It touched me so deeply the first time I listened that all I could do was cry."

Then, Rachelle invited Casi to church. Casi spent a couple weeks listening to those sermons before deciding to go to church. "I'm not sure why, but I was scared to go," Casi shared. However, Rachelle made Casi feel comfortable and Casi chose to go.

"When I was in high school, I went to a youth group at a local church," said Casi. "It was good, except we didn't learn that much. We went to church, sang in the church, and learned the routine. But I didn't understand the whole thing and what God has done for me! At some point, I stopped going to church. I hadn't gone for about 5 years, before coming to Victory Church."

"It is here at Victory Church that I finally understood what God did for me. I am now saved through the blood Jesus shed for me!"

Casi's story continues... CDs help more friends and family find Christ!

Sometimes talking to our closest friends and relatives is even more difficult than sharing our faith with a perfect stranger. Casi was working at an insurance agency with her sister and a very good friend. "My sister and friend had fallen out of going to church too," said Casi. "I needed to share with them how God had changed my life." She decided to use the same strategy that Rachelle had used with her. Casi played recordings of Pastor Josh's sermons at work for her sister and friend, plus she gave them copies of their own to listen to at their leisure.

Now they all go to Victory Church, praising God together, worshipping together, and growing together.

"Everyone needs to hear the word of God," Casi continued. "People like me, my sister, and our friend wouldn't be here, if it weren't for messages on CD. My life has changed tremendously, and I thank God for that!" 🐚

Application

Ask the Lord to help you form friendships and new connections as you go through daily life. May the Lord help you to consider others as more important than yourself. Look for opportunities to share your faith with your friends and those you meet. Make sure to have CDs and recorded messages with you as you go throughout your day.

Daily Journal

Today's Date_____

Write down ideas of how you may be able to share the good news of the Gospel with your friends.

_____

_____

_____

_____

What opportunities have you had recently to share your faith?

_____

_____

_____

_____

Please write your prayer for today. Ask the Lord to help you build friendships and connections with those you meet during daily life. And, ask the Lord to touch the hearts and lives of your friends.

_____

_____

_____

_____

Day #9 – Acquaintances

ach of us has people that we would consider acquaintances. These may be people we have just met or people we do not know well enough to consider a friend. Or, some of our acquaintances may even be people that we will become friends with in the future. We may not even know that a particular acquaintance may become a good friend in the future.

Over the years, I have heard countless stories of people finding Christ through an acquaintance. The Lord may bring someone into your life or across your path at just the right time so that you can have an eternal impact.

Power Thought for Today

In looking at the life of Jesus, he shared with those that he came across in daily life. There are stories of Jesus sharing with a woman at a well, people he met along the road, and even people he encountered at the temple.

"When a Samaritan woman came to draw water, Jesus said to her, 'Will you give me a drink?' (His disciples had gone into the town to buy food.)

The Samaritan woman said to him, 'You are a Jew and I am a Samaritan woman. How can you ask me for a drink? (For Jews do not associate with Samaritans.)

Jesus answered her, 'If you knew the gift of God and who it is that asks you for a drink, you would have asked him and he would have given you living water.'" — John 4:7-10 (NIV)

Pray that the Lord would help you to point those you come across in daily life to the fountain of living water – Jesus!

Student helps a fellow classmate find Christ and a church!

Jessica was in the same college class as a fellow student named Julie. She did not know Julie that well, but she saw her at class. One day, Jessica gave Julie a CD of her pastor's sermon. The CD opened the door for Jessica to give Julie an invitation to church, and the CD helped Julie to feel comfortable with the church. It was not long before Julie decided to visit the church. After Julie went to church a couple times, she made a commitment to Christ and was baptized soon after. Jessica and

Julie ended up becoming good friends, and Jessica helped Julie grow in her new faith.

A man working at a gas station is saved!

David worked at a gas station with a mini-mart convenience store. During this time, he had a regular customer who came in to buy coffee each day. The customer ended up giving David messages from her church and invited him to church. One message was a Thanksgiving message on giving thanks. After several invitations, David agreed to check out the church. He had a Sunday off from work and visited the church. Before too long, for some reason he started getting his Sundays off regularly. Just a few weeks later, David made a commitment to Christ.

One of the neatest parts about this story is that on the day David made a commitment to Christ, he shared his faith with someone before he even left the church parking lot! When David was walking out of church, he saw a car broken down at the edge of the church parking lot. These people with the broken car did not attend the church. David went over to help the people with their vehicle and ended up giving them a copy of a sermon. Just minutes after making a commitment to Christ, David was able to share his new faith with others!

For David, this was just the beginning of developing a lifestyle of sharing his faith. Now, David regularly shares his faith by talking to the people he meets and by giving away copies of the sermons he hears at church.

Application

Ask the Lord to open your eyes to the people around you who need to find Christ. Look and pray for opportunities to share with those around you. The Lord may use you to have a life-changing impact on those you meet. In the story above, David shared his faith just minutes after becoming a Christian! And remember, anyone can share a recorded message.

Daily Journal

Do you have any acquaintances that the Lord may be leading you to share the Gospel with? If so, write down their names.

_____

_____

_____

_____

What opportunities have you had recently to share your faith?

_____

_____

_____

_____

Please write your prayer for today. Ask the Lord to open your eyes to those around you who need to hear the Gospel. Ask the Lord for opportunities to share the Gospel with them.

_____

_____

_____

_____

_____

Day #10 – Restaurants: Taking the Gospel With You When You Eat

estaurants are one of the many places where we encounter other people. Over the years, I have heard story after story of people being reached at restaurants.

The environment in restaurants makes it a natural place to talk to people. I have heard of many people getting into spiritual conversations with the waiter or waitress. And, it is very easy to leave a CD message with your tip. Just be sure to leave a good tip too! The next time you go out to eat don't miss an opportunity to share the Gospel.

Power Thought for Today

The next time you go out to eat be sure to think about spiritual food as well. Your waiter or waitress may have followed Christ at some point in time or may have never heard the Gospel even once. By giving a CD to your waiter or waitress, you will create an opportunity for the Gospel to be heard.

"So then faith comes by hearing, and hearing by the word of God."
– Romans 10:17 (NKJV)

A waitress saved...

One man, a pastor, regularly ate at the same restaurant after church on Sunday. He started giving the waitress a copy of the message each Sunday. After the waitress received a few messages, she began to look forward to the messages and appreciated receiving them on a regular basis. Before too long, the waitress and her boyfriend came to church one Sunday. The boyfriend gave his life to Christ and the waitress recommitted her life to Christ. They decided to live life God's way. This couple committed their lives to Christ, and they committed their lives to each other by getting married.

This all happened because one man faithfully shared messages with the waitress at the restaurant his family frequently ate at after church on Sundays.

Woman receives Gospel message at a restaurant...

Here's a story that my father, Johnny Berguson, shared with me and others not too long ago...

"You can give messages to people you don't know that well. I was having supper with my wife at a Mexican restaurant about 40 miles away from our home. The waitress came over to the table. She said, 'Hi, my name is…. and I didn't quite understand what she said her name was. But it's part of her job to say her first name and to say 'I'll be your waitress tonight.' I said, 'Pardon me, but I didn't quite catch your name.' She was surprised that I cared enough to know her name.

"She opened up a little bit and started to talk. I thought I should ask her another question now and then, while she was waiting on us. We got into a conversation, and I found out that she was very interested in horses and her mother was interested in horses as well. It's amazing the things the Lord can work out so that you can talk to someone. How in the world I ever got into a conversation about horses, I, to this day, do not know. In any event, I said to her, 'I have a recorded message that might be very helpful. It's on horse psychology.'

"She didn't know this, but I've trained horses according to Biblical principles for child rearing, and I made this recording years ago. So I offered it to her and her mother. Along with this message I gave her another message called 'The Greatest Horse Training Secret I've Ever Learned.' In this special message, I share the greatest horse training secret I've ever learned. It's found in the book of James. *'If any of you lacks wisdom let him ask of God who gives generously to all men.'* I relate this principle to horse training, but I also relate it to all of life as well. This leads me into sharing my Christian testimony on this message. The waitress was very grateful to receive these two messages. For many years, I heard from at least a dozen people a year who came to the Lord through that second message.

"I find it incredible. God uses CD's, tapes, MP3s, and recorded messages to touch people's lives. God prepares people's hearts, and they come to the Lord through hearing these messages even when you're not there."

Application

You can share the Gospel with people you do not know very well. Restaurants are a unique place to talk with people you may have never met or do not know very well. You never know, you may be the only connection with the Gospel that these people will ever have.

Pray that the Lord would bring people across your path that He would have you to meet. Ask the Lord to create common points of interest in conversations and give you opportunities to share the Gospel. Pray that the Lord would help you to care about people like He cares about them.

Daily Journal

What ideas and strategies can you use to reach those you come in contact with at public places such as restaurants?

_____

_____

_____

What opportunities have you had recently to share your faith?

_____

_____

_____

Please write your prayer for today. Ask the Lord to direct conversations with those you meet to points of connection and spiritual matters. Pray for divine appointments and connections. Ask the Lord to help you in sharing the Gospel with these people.

_____

_____

_____

_____

_____

Day #11 – POWER DAY – Fishbowls and Fishing for Souls

Power Days: On power days, you will learn how to extend and multiply your impact. Power Days will show you how to increase your outreach impact in your community, how you can help your church multiply its effectiveness, or how to multiply your own personal outreach efforts.

O ver the past several days, you have been learning how to reach the people you know and meet. Today, you will learn how you can impact the lives of people you have never met and may never meet. All you need is a fishbowl and some messages.

> *Today, you will learn how you can impact the lives of people you have never met and may never meet. All you need is a fishbowl and some messages.*

⚡ **Power Thought for Today**

You can help to saturate your community with the Gospel. Fishbowl outreach is one of the simplest strategies that you can use to help spread the Gospel in your community. Seek God to see if He would have you to multiply your outreach efforts through fishbowl outreach. If your church already uses fishbowls, you may be able to help with this ministry or add fishbowls to new locations. If you work at an office, you may be able to keep a fishbowl on your desk! Or, God may put it on your heart for you to start a fishbowl outreach ministry for your church.

"... the kingdom of heaven is like a net that was let down into the lake and caught all kinds of fish."   – Matthew 13:47 (NIV)

A waitress saved...

The basic strategy is to use fishbowls to go fishing, spiritually speaking. That's right! You can use fishbowls to reach people you have never met and will likely never meet.

The concept is so simple... Simply fill fishbowls with CDs and recorded messages. Then, ask restaurants, gas stations, convenience stores, doctor's offices, and other shops if you can leave a fishbowl at their store. Most stores will give you permission to put the fishbowls near the cash register. Each fishbowl should have a sign that says something like "FREE! TAKE ONE!" or "FREE! Food for Your Soul." If you are too shy to get permission to leave fishbowls at stores, team up with a friend who is outgoing.

When you get your fishbowls, be sure to get fishbowls with a wide enough "mouth" that the CDs will fit inside the fishbowls. See below for where you can find specially designed outreach fishbowls.[1] Once you put the fishbowls out, check back regularly to see if it is time to refill the fishbowls. Fishbowls are a fun and creative outreach strategy!

This lady has inspired many to reach others for Christ!

The fishbowl concept originally came from a woman named Darlene Presley in North Carolina. She had always thought of others being used by God and wondered how God would use her. She did not know it, but God was going to use Darlene in a very special way.

Darlene discovered one way God was going to use her when she was in a nursing home visiting her grandmother. As she looked around, she noticed many people that had been forgotten. She started giving messages to these forgotten people and their friends. One day in church she said, "Salvation is free, you cannot put a price on it." The Lord was growing her heart for the lost and those in need.

She wanted a way to distribute messages to *everyone* in the community. One day while she was shopping she found what she was looking for – fishbowls! She purchased several of them and filled them with messages. Then, she labeled them "Food for Your Soul." Darlene placed the fishbowls in local restaurants, convenience stores, and gas stations. She replenishes the fishbowls every Monday morning.

Darlene says that many people are afraid to go to an unfamiliar church. Through CDs and recorded messages, people can discover what the church is like before attending. Darlene describes her work as, "Breaking down the barriers and opening doors to Christ."

One man helps launch fishbowl outreach that brings many people to church!

A man in Virginia named Calvin says that fishbowls have brought a lot of new members to his church. Twenty to thirty copies of messages are made each week and are used to fill two fishbowls that are placed in the community. "I read about it and thought, man, this is too simple, but it's pretty cool. The more I read, I knew

---

[1] When buying fishbowls, it is important to get special wide-mouth fishbowls that can hold CDs. Go to 40DaysToFruitfulness.com to find a research link to inexpensive wide-mouth fishbowls and fishbowl outreach kits.

God was saying to me, 'You can do this!'" The next day Calvin ordered a couple of fishbowls.

With the fishbowls, Calvin got a "FREE Food for Your Soul" mini-sign. This sign gave him an idea – he could put fishbowls at the grocery store! Calvin got permission from the owner, and every Sunday the fishbowl in the grocery market is refilled with 21 copies of the last sermon. "When I came in recently on Thursday, there were three left," he went on. "Often it's empty. The workers there tell me some customers get upset if they come in and the bowl is empty!"

Wherever Calvin's pastor goes, the pastor hears "I get your messages from a fishbowl." A lot of new members have joined the church because one man cared enough to help his church through the use of fishbowl ministry.

A fishbowl in a flower shop helps husband find Christ!

One Christian, who owned a flower shop, placed a fishbowl in the flower shop. A man came into this shop to buy flowers for his wife. This man's wife was a Christian who regularly told him about God and prayed for him. The husband took a message and came back to the flower shop about two weeks later. He told the flower shop owner that he had committed his life to Christ after listening to that message.

Application

Ask God for wisdom if you should start a fishbowl ministry or develop some other community outreach effort to share Gospel messages. If God lays this on your heart, then do it. Pray that God would touch the hearts of the people who listen to the messages. Pray that those who need to take the messages would find them.

Daily Journal

Today's Date_____

What ideas and strategies can you use to reach your community? In what locations might you be able to utilize fishbowls?

_____

_____

_____

What opportunities have you had recently to share your faith?

_____

_____

_____

_____

Please write your prayer for today. Pray and ask the Lord for wisdom regarding whether you should get involved in fishbowl ministry. Ask God to give you wisdom and creative ideas in reaching your community for Christ.

_____

_____

_____

_____

Day #12 – HELP!!!! What if I'm shy???... Part I

The Bible is filled with stories of all different personality types. God uses all different types of people to advance His kingdom. Some people are outgoing such as Peter, who often spoke without thinking. Others are shy or fearful. After Jesus' death, the disciples were so scared that they hid in fear. Later, God gave them boldness, and they proclaimed the good news of the Gospel.

With the principles in this book, even shy people are sharing their faith. Shy people are becoming some of the most effective evangelists with CDs and recorded messages.

Power Thought for Today

Bold or shy, God can use you. You do not have to have a special personality type to be used by God. Throughout the ages, God has used all different types of people. God can use you - even if you're shy - to produce lots of good fruit!

"But he who received seed on the good ground is he who hears the word and understands it, who indeed bears fruit and produces: some a hundredfold, some sixty, some thirty."   – Matthew 13:23 (NKJV)

Shy lady able to share messages...

Ann Spangler of North Park Church has spent years and years working in her church's message ministry. "I've never felt comfortable carrying on a conversation where I'm digging into where a person is at spiritually," Ann shared. "I care about it, but it has been hard for me to develop. I do feel comfortable handing people [messages]."

There are people that we all come in contact with every day that need the peace and joy that a relationship with Christ can give. When Ann sees someone hurting or in need, she simply offers a message and kind words such as: "I understand the situation you're in. I feel for you. My pastor just gave us a message on a subject that you might find beneficial."

Ann shared a story of a visitor who came to church. He had been very intrigued by the recorded message he received. Later, the man became an active member of the church and joined the message ministry team.

53

Even 5-year olds can share messages!

At a Baptist church in Virginia, the CD ministry turns every member into a preacher. If even a 5-year old can be an evangelist, then anyone be an evangelist! Recently, a little girl was leaving this church with five CDs. When asked why she had them, she cheerfully replied, "My teachers like them!" This five-year old is doing her part in fulfilling the Great Commission!

Application

Pray and ask the Lord to give you boldness and to help you find a way to reach out even if you are shy. Fortunately, even shy people can give out messages to strangers. It is very easy to tell someone that you have a gift for them. Nearly everyone appreciates receiving a gift.

Or perhaps you do not have an ounce of "shyness" in you, but you know someone who does. Encourage your shy friend to share their faith using CDs and recorded messages!

Today's Date_____

What is your personality like? Are you shy or outgoing? How do you think God can use you to reach others for Christ?

_____

_____

_____

_____

What opportunities have you had recently to share your faith?

_____

_____

_____

_____

Please write your prayer for today. Pray for opportunities to share the message of the Gospel with others. Ask the Lord to give you boldness and creativity in sharing your faith with others.

_____

_____

_____

_____

Day #13 – HELP!!!! What if I'm shy??? Part II

There is good news about being shy! If you consider yourself shy, you may be in good company. A lot of people you will be reaching out to also consider themselves to be shy. According to research, almost half of the population consider themselves to be shy.[2] So, if you are shy, you really are in good company!

Just as initiating a conversation with someone might be intimidating, think about the person on the other end. They may feel too shy to talk very much! But, they will probably gladly accept a CD to listen to.

Power Thought for Today

Ask God to give you creative ways to share the Gospel through CDs and recorded messages. Today's story is about a lady that is very shy, but she found a way to give out 20 to 30 messages per week.

You don't have to be outgoing to share the Gospel. You just have to be faithful!

"...The harvest is plentiful, but the workers are few. Ask the Lord of the harvest, therefore, to send out workers into his harvest field."

– Luke 10:2 (NIV)

Lady too shy to talk leads 18 people to Christ!

At Pastor David Miller's church there was a shy lady. This woman felt she could not witness with her own mouth, but she used messages to lead 18 people to Christ! She was shy, but she did not allow her shyness to hold her back in giving out audio messages. She has made giving away messages a lifestyle. If you saw her today, you would probably see her walking out of church with a stack of CDs to give away!

Shy woman finds a creative way to share the Gospel with 20 to 30 people each week!

One of the members at Cornerstone Bible Church works at a local food bank. This woman was so energized by the idea of sharing the Word that she asked for

[2] *Psychology Today.* http://www.psychologytoday.com/articles/pto-1240.html.

permission to put copies of her pastor's message in with the food packages. She is very shy, but this is a way for her to reach out into her community and impact lives for Christ. She is thrilled to be giving out about 20 to 30 messages each week. There are many ways in which even the shyest person can share the word of God with their community – you just have to look for the opportunities that God provides! 🐝

Application

If you consider yourself to be a shy person, you are in good company. If you are outgoing, perhaps you can help others get activated in sharing messages. Ask the Lord to give you creative ideas in reaching others for Christ.

If you do you not feel that you are truly activated into the harvest, ask the Lord to 'send you out' as a worker into the harvest field!

Daily Journal

You might have some creative ideas for sharing 10, 20, 30 or more CDs and recorded messages each week. Please write down any ideas you have and ask God for wisdom.

_____

_____

_____

_____

What opportunities have you had recently to share your faith?

_____

_____

_____

Please write your prayer for today. Pray and ask the Lord to 'send you out' and activate you as a worker into the harvest field.

_____

_____

_____

_____

_____

Day #14 – Witnessing Two By Two

In the New Testament, people regularly shared their faith and reached out to others in teams of two or more. As you continue to work on developing a lifestyle of outreach, connect with others who share your same heart for outreach.

Just imagine having several friends who share your passion for reaching the lost. When you spend time with these friends and encounter other people, you may even find unexpected opportunities to share the Gospel.

Power Thought for Today

When you reach out to people who want to hear about Christ, there is multiplied impact when you do this with a fellow believer. God has created us to function with other believers. Jesus sent out his twelve disciples two-by-two to minister, and then he later sent out the seventy two-by-two.

"After these things the Lord appointed seventy others also, and sent them two by two before His face into every city and place where He Himself was about to go. Then He said to them, 'The harvest truly is great..."
— Luke 10:1-2a (NKJV)

Two by two – Two powerful opportunities to share CDs!

Two ladies attended a business and communications conference. On the last day of the conference one of the ladies forgot her notebook in her hotel room. She had already checked out of her room, so she had to find someone to let her back into the room. A bellhop agreed to let her back into her room.

As she was going back to her room in the elevator, she asked the bellhop where he was from. The bellhop said that he had moved to Atlanta from New York City a good while back. He said he had a new granddaughter born on September 9, 2001, just before 9/11. The bellhop was supposed to be in the World Trade Center on 9/11. Instead, this gentleman was with his granddaughter on that day. Immediately after hearing his story, the lady told the bellhop that she believed God had saved his life for a reason. The bellhop seemed unsure of this, but this comment seemed to really get him thinking.

When the lady went back to the conference, the speaker was talking about the importance of family and the importance of prioritizing family. During a question and answer segment, the lady shared the story of what had just happened with the bellhop. The bellhop would have been in the World Trade Center on the day it collapsed, if he would not have been with his family. The story fit perfectly with the speaker's message and really touched the attendees.

Right after the session ended, the lady started talking to a man from India. She asked him if he was a Christian. He replied that he thought all religions were the same. This quickly opened up a dialogue between the two of them. The other lady heard the discussion and went across the room. She got two CDs, including *"Listen to the Bible in One Hour,"* from her luggage. She walked back over to the other lady and the man from India, who were still engaged in the discussion. She handed the man from India the two CDs and told him that they were a gift. He was very appreciative.

Shortly after this discussion, the two ladies walked downstairs to the hotel lobby. They were surprised to find the same bellhop. The lady who had talked to the bellhop earlier shared that she had just told his story to the entire conference! She once again affirmed that she believed that God had saved his life for a reason. This time, the bellhop agreed that God had saved his life for a reason. While the discussion was taking place, the other lady got another two CDs out of the luggage to give to the bellhop as a gift. The bellhop was very thankful for the gift.

As the two ladies were leaving the hotel, they both felt like the bellhop was going to give his life to Christ. The bellhop had really been touched by the events of that day. The ladies knew they had been on a special mission from God that day.

These two ladies worked together two by two. One talked and the other shared the messages on CD. They worked together as a team.

Application

Find a "power friend." Seek out a friend who wants to make reaching the lost a lifestyle. Ask the Lord to help you find "power friends" that energize you and partner with you in the reaching out to others. Pray for the Lord to help you find friends that help multiply your impact for God's kingdom.

Daily Journal

Who are some possible "power friends" who might partner with you in sharing the Gospel with others? Write down their names.

_____

_____

_____

What opportunities have you had recently to share your faith?

_____

_____

_____

Please write your prayer for today. Ask God to help you to find "power friends." Talk to the people that God places on your heart, and ask these friends to join with you in going out "two by two" to share the Gospel.

_____

_____

_____

_____

_____

Day #15 – Types of Messages – Sermons

In today's segment you will discover many different types of messages that you can share with people. Different messages will be more effective in reaching different people. There are countless messages that you can share with people.

One of the messages that you can give away on a regular basis is your pastor's weekly sermon. Simply get copies of the sermon each week and give them away as you encounter people who might benefit from listening to the message. Many faithful church attendees also listen to the sermon again so they can both remember and apply the sermon. You would be surprised how much more of the sermon you can retain just by listening to the message a second time.

You can help take the message beyond the four walls of the church. Pray that God would show you people who need to hear the sermon.

Power Thought for Today

The Lord has given your pastor a message, not just for your church, but for your community. When your pastor preaches from the Bible and reads from the Scriptures, this is the Word of God going forth. You can take God's message preached from the pulpit into your community. God has promised that when His Word goes forth that it will not return void.

"For as the rain comes down, and the snow from heaven, and do not return there, but water the earth, and make it bring forth and bud, That it may give seed to the sower and bread to the eater, So shall My word be that goes forth from My mouth; It shall not return to Me void, but it shall accomplish what I please, And it shall prosper in the thing for which I sent it."
– Isaiah 55:10-11 (NKJV, emphasis added)

Sermon messages help this woman find Christ!

A lady named Marilyn in Vermont started giving her friend Judy copies of her pastor's sermons. Each time she would listen to the messages she started to weep and did not know why she was weeping. Just a few days after listening to one of the sermons, Judy met with Marilyn and her pastor. Judy asked why she started crying each time she heard the messages. The pastor explained that this was the Holy Spirit moving on Judy's heart. Judy made Jesus her Lord and Savior that day.

Today, Judy now shares sermon messages to reach others for Christ. Judy's own life has been blessed, and she wants to bless the lives of others. Judy praises God for the impact of recorded messages and her new life in Christ!

CDs and recorded sermons are touching lives for eternity!

There are countless stories of lives that have been impacted for eternity just by sharing the weekly sermon with a friend or stranger. Here are seven powerful stories from this book of people whose lives have been touched by sermons:

1. A lady in England named Marion was planning to commit suicide until her friend boxed up some sermons from her pastor and sent them to Marion. Marion found new life in Christ. (Day 3)
2. A young girl helped her father find Christ by sending him sermon messages, even though he lived in another state! (Day 4)
3. A man named Randall mailed his brother recorded messages for twelve years, and his brother found Christ through these messages. Many sermon messages and the U.S. Postal Service helped this man find Christ through the convicting power of the Holy Spirit. (Day 4)
4. Sermon messages helped a waitress and her boyfriend find Christ. The waitress was given a copy of the sermon each week. (Day 10)
5. Sermon messages traveled from person to person through seven floors of an office building. (Day 6)
6. A man was saved in his basement as he listened to sermons from a local pastor. These audio messages were left in his basement by a friend. (Day 7)
7. And, a lady found a church through a sermon on CD. (Day 8)

CDs and recorded sermons are touching lives every day! Lives are being impacted for eternity as the Word of God as preached from pulpit is going out into communities.

Application

Sermon messages can be a great resource to add to your toolbox. Simply start picking up CD copies of the sermon each week and then give them away to those God brings across your path. It is very easy to say to a friend or stranger, "I heard a message at church that touched me. I'd like to give you a copy of the message." Or, as you listen to a sermon being preached, the Lord may lay on your heart someone who needs to hear that sermon. Simply share something like, "You came to mind when I heard this message, and I thought you might like to listen to it."

Daily Journal

What people do you know who you might be able to give a copy of your pastor's sermon to each week or from time to time?

_____

_____

_____

_____

What opportunities have you had recently to share your faith?

_____

_____

_____

_____

Please write your prayer for today. Pray and ask the Lord to give you opportunities to share copies of the sermons each week.

_____

_____

_____

_____

_____

Day #16 – Power Day – Messages-To-Go℠

hen churches make copies of their weekly sermons available immediately after the service for people to take with them when they go home, this is called Messages-To-Go℠. Yesterday, you learned about the impact of sermon messages. There are countless stories of lives that have been touched for eternity as sermons have been taken beyond the four walls of the church. These messages on CDs, tapes, MP3s, and DVDs are having an impact on souls.

If your church does not presently have a Messages-To-Go℠ Ministry, you may be able to help your church get a Message-To-Go Ministry started. Or, if your church already has this ministry, you may be able to help extend the reach of the Messages-To-Go ministry. A Messages-To-Go ministry can help multiply the impact of your entire church.

Power Thought for Today

When a church catches a vision for taking the sermon beyond the four walls of the church into the community, this can literally multiply the church's impact.

Ordinary Christians and churches are multiplying the impact of their entire church with Messages-To-Go Ministries. CDs and recorded messages of the weekly sermons are made available after each service for people to take with them. Each message is like a seed being planted.

In order to reap a bountiful harvest, you and your church need to sow a lot of "seeds." Only God knows the conditions of the hearts of men and women. Pray that your seeds will find a lot of good soil in the hearts of the hearers.

"Then he (Jesus) told them many things in parables, saying: 'A farmer went out to sow his seed. As he was scattering the seed, <u>some fell along the path</u>, and the birds came and ate it up. <u>Some fell on rocky places</u>, where it did not have much soil. It sprang up quickly, because the soil was shallow. But when the sun came up, the plants were scorched, and they withered because they had no root. <u>Other seed fell among thorns</u>, which grew up and choked the plants. <u>Still other seed fell on good soil, where it produced a crop—a hundred, sixty or thirty times what was sown</u>. He who has ears, let him hear.'"

– Matthew 13:3-9 (NIV, emphasis added)

Church adds 75 to 100 members through Messages-To-Go℠ Ministry!

After adding a Messages-To-Go Ministry, Union Baptist Church started growing so fast they had a difficult time learning everyone's names. The church grew by over 60% in four years. "Yeah, in fact my wife, the technical 'wiz,' asked the church to purchase a digital camera to take photos on Sunday of those who joined," said Pastor Calvin Nunnally. He continued, "We were adding members faster than we could learn their names!"

What draws the visitors? "Some listen to the sermon again themselves," the pastor said. "And there are a few collectors – they have every [message] we've ever made! But by far, most people tell us there is someone they know who needs to hear that day's message. Quite a few people take several copies to give away!"

Pastor leads his congregation by example!

Pastor Cook in Florida leads his congregation by example. He keeps 5 to 10 copies of outreach CDs in his car at all times. Pastor Cook's personal goal is to hand out 5 to 15 CDs each week. He hands them out at places like Wal-Mart, Home Depot, and the bank.

Pastor Cook's church grew from 130 people to 200 people in one year. Before the CD ministry only 15% of the congregation was actively sharing their faith. Now, 30-35% of congregation is giving out at least one CD a week. Over 80% of the church has given out at least one CD to a lost person.

Church adds 1,300+ people in two years after starting Messages-To-Go Ministry!

Christ Community Church grew to over 2,200 people after it added its Messages-To-Go Ministry. Pastor Steve Boyer attributes much of the growth to people taking and giving away messages. He says that this has been "grass roots" evangelism at its best. Typical of most churches, the donations received as people take CDs more than covers the cost of the ministry. Christ Community Church continues to distribute thousands and thousands of CDs each year and is touching more and more lives.

Dying church grows from 15 to 180 in twenty-four months!

A fire has been ignited in the hearts of the congregation at Goshen Baptist Church to see the lost saved. The church, pastored by Scott Reese, has equipped their congregation to take CDs and recorded messages into their community. People often leave with a stack of five or more messages on a given Sunday. This congregation is both praying and putting their prayers into action by giving out messages. For 40 consecutive weeks, this church saw at least one decision for Christ made each week!

Application

Your church needs an *army* of Christians who consistently and lovingly present the Gospel to as many people as possible. A Messages-To-Go Ministry can help your church build this army and equip it with tools. Ordinary Christians have been able to help multiply the impact of their entire church by helping their church get a Messages-To-Go ministry started. You can be part of this army.

If your church does not have a Messages-To-Go ministry, pray and ask the Lord if He would want you to help your church get a Messages-To-Go Ministry started. Your church may need finances to start a Messages-To-Go ministry or someone to lead the ministry. Perhaps, the Lord would have you to donate to this ministry or volunteer your time. Pray and ask God for wisdom.

And, be sure to take CDs and recorded messages of your pastor's sermons into your community. Your pastor has a message not just for your church – but your entire community!

Daily Journal

How does a Messages-To-Go℠ ministry benefit a church?

_____

_____

_____

_____

What opportunities have you had recently to share your faith?

_____

_____

_____

_____

Please write your prayer for today. Pray and ask the Lord for wisdom in regards to if He would have you to play a role in activating or expanding the Messages-To-Go℠ Ministry at your church.

_____

_____

_____

_____

_____

Day #17 – Prison – The Gospel Goes to Prison

n the Scriptures, it says that Jesus came to set the captives free. Many young men and women are ending up behind bars in today's world. Recorded messages and prison outreach ministries are helping many of these people to find freedom in Christ. Although these people may be in a physical prison, they can find freedom for their souls through Christ.

It doesn't matter where on earth a person goes; the Lord can still find them there. Even if a person ends up on death row, the Lord can find them.

Power Thought for Today

The Lord can use you to reach people you might not ever think you would have an opportunity to reach. Regardless of where people go, they cannot get so far away from God that He is too far away to reach them.

"Where can I go from Your Spirit?
Or where can I flee from Your presence?
If I ascend into heaven, You are there;
If I make my bed in hell, behold, You are there..."
— Psalm 139:7-8 (NKJV)

Man reached in prison on death row!

A church in Maryland has recorded their morning and evening services, as well as their Tuesday-evening Bible teachings, for years. One of those teachings, passing from friend to friend, made it to a death-row inmate in Illinois. This man, now a Christian, wrote the church to request additional messages, which he then shared with other Christians there in his penitentiary. These teaching-oriented messages gave the men comfort, instruction, and perspective to face life – and even death – in prison.

Another man, also a death-row prisoner in that same prison, became increasingly unsettled about his readiness to face eternity. "I've got to have whatever you have," he told one of the Christian inmates. They began to tell him about Jesus. He too began listening to the messages from the Maryland church. After listening to some messages, he also decided to consider the claims of Christ.

Lady reached in prison through recorded message!

A young woman in Newport News, Virginia, had been put in jail for substance abuse. A church in the area recorded its pastor's sermons and broadcast them over a local radio station.

This inmate heard the pre-recorded messages and began corresponding with the church. She also phoned the church and was ministered to by the receptionist. The pastor and others prayed with her and counseled her.

When she was released, she visited the church. She committed her life to Christ and was baptized. She has turned away from drugs and continues to receive spiritual nourishment from both live sermons and recorded messages.

Application

Pray that the Lord causes the messages you give out to travel to the places where people need Christ. Each message you give out may travel from person to person and may end up being listened to by people you may never even meet. The typical CD message is passed along to three or four people. Some messages are passed along to dozens of people. There are stories of some CDs traveling across the country.

The typical CD message is passed along to three or four people.

Special note: It is also important to note that prisons have restrictions on the types of recorded media that can be allowed in particular prisons. If you are going to send or distribute messages to prisoners, find out which types of recorded media are allowable in that prison.

Daily Journal

Can you think of any new or unusual places where you can give out messages or share the Gospel?

_____

_____

_____

What opportunities have you had recently to share your faith?

_____

_____

_____

_____

Please write your prayer for today. Pray that the messages you give out would travel to the places where people need to hear the Gospel. And, ask God to cause you to meet people who need to hear the Gospel.

_____

_____

_____

_____

_____

Day #18 – Listen to the Bible in One Hour

here are all different types of recorded messages that you can give away. As you continue your journey toward greater fruitfulness, you will learn about more and more types of messages that you can give away. One of my personal favorite messages to give away is the *Listen to the Bible in One Hour* CD. This audio is a collection of Scripture verses from Genesis through the New Testament that gives a good overview of the Bible and salvation. The best thing about this audio message is that it contains only Scripture verses! There is no preaching on this CD, only Scripture verses — it is very powerful.

This recording is a lot of fun to give away, because it is very unique. There are a lot of people who would like to learn more about the Bible, and this gives them a quick overview in less than one hour. I enjoy listening to this CD personally too. It is a great little tool.

"For the word of God is living and active. Sharper than any double-edged sword, it penetrates even to dividing soul and spirit, joints and marrow; it judges the thoughts and attitudes of the heart. Nothing in all creation is hidden from God's sight. Everything is uncovered and laid bare before the eyes of him to whom we must give account."

– Hebrews 4:12-13 (NIV)

Power Thought for Today

As you get more and more committed to outreach as a lifestyle, you will begin to collect resources to help you. CDs like *Listen to the Bible in One Hour* are the types of CDs and recorded messages you should be looking to add to your toolbox. Just as farmers and fisherman use different tools and equipment for different activities, your own collection of tools for outreach should begin to grow. You will end up giving out different CDs and recorded messages to different people. The messages may even change depending on what time of year it is or if there is a holiday.

Listen to the Bible CD inspires man to start "reading" the Bible...

A man went to a rental car company. As he was picking up his rental car, he got into a conversation. He ended up talking to a husband and wife. He ended up giving them copies of *Listen to the Bible in One Hour*. One wanted a tape and the other wanted a CD. They gladly accepted the messages.

When the traveler returned the car, he ended up talking to the husband again. He asked him if he had listened to the CD yet. He said he had not listened to it yet, but he was going to listen to it – and he and his wife had already started reading the Bible together. Just being given a CD inspired this man to read the Bible with his wife. Wow! This man's life was being impacted before even listening to the message.

Chinese businessman gives outreach messages away – prior to even becoming a Christian!

One man told the story of a Chinese businessman named Jim that he has known for several years. Over the years, this businessman has shared his faith with Jim on several occasions. During a recent visit, the businessman gave Jim three copies of the CD, *Listen to the Bible in One Hour*. Jim was very appreciative of the CDs.

When the man saw Jim the next time, he asked him if he still had the *Listen to the Bible in One Hour* CDs. He said that he had given all three of the CDs away! Jim is not even a Christian *yet*, and he gave all the outreach CDs to others. So, the businessman gave Jim six more CDs, and he asked Jim to be sure to keep one for himself. Jim is a very generous man!

Before Jim left, the businessman prayed with him. He asked God to bless Jim's trip back to China and to keep Jim safe. After Jim returned home, Jim called the man and thanked him for praying for his trip. The businessman is seeing changes in Jim, and he is believing God for Jim's salvation.

Sick pets lead to outreach opportunity

Johnny Berguson (my father) took his dog to the local vet clinic for an appointment. While there, he gave a lady a copy of the *Listen to the Bible in One Hour* CD and other people in the office started asking for copies too. He soon ran out of copies to give people in the vet clinic! It is amazing how people love to receive CDs!

Kids take CDs to give to teachers!

At the end of the school year, a 9-year old girl wanted to give her teachers a gift. So, she asked at church if she could have two *Listen to the Bible in One Hour* CDs to give to her teachers. The church had several copies so they offered one to each of the students at Children's Church. That same week, there were two children visiting from several hours away. The children visiting the church got very excited about giving away CDs, and they wanted more than one copy. They asked for several copies so they could give them away to as many people as possible. Through that one request from a young girl, the church was able to hand out more than 20 CDs in many parts of their state! ❦

Application

Ask the Lord to give you wisdom as you build your toolbox for outreach. Pray for wisdom in selecting messages to be part of your outreach toolbox. Sermons, testimonies, and special messages are common messages for outreach.

If you would like to get *Listen to the Bible in One Hour*, you can get a copy. See the resources at the end of this book.[3] Or, perhaps, your church already has copies of this CD available that you can pick up.

And the best part is, when you get a "master" copy of *Listen to the Bible in One Hour* you can use it to make as many copies as you want for outreach purposes! This recording is a FreeAccess Master™ meaning that you have permission to make copies for outreach purposes. Learn more about Free Access Masters™ on the website.

---

[3] Go to www.40DaysToFruitfulness.com to get the *Listen to the Bible in One Hour* CD.

Daily Journal

What messages would you like to add to your outreach toolbox?

_____

_____

_____

_____

What opportunities have you had recently to share your faith?

_____

_____

_____

_____

Please write your prayer for today. Ask the Lord to help as you select messages for your outreach toolbox. And, pray for opportunities to share your faith with others.

_____

_____

_____

_____

_____

Day #19 – Life Stories

Life Stories are another important category of messages for outreach. Life Story messages are exactly that – Life Stories. They tend to be life stories of famous people, people with exciting life stories, and life stories of professional athletes.

There is a whole collection of life story messages available from people including Joni Eareckson Tada, Chuck Colson, and the baseball pitcher Dave Dravecky. Or, you can develop your own collection life story messages.

Power Thought for Today

Lives are impacted as the stories of others are shared. Just think about those whose life stories have impacted your own life. You can use life story messages both for your own personal growth and for outreach.

In my own life, I can still remember powerful life stories I heard when I was child. One time, a missionary came to church that had been in a prisoner-of-war camp. He had been a prisoner in Russia, and he became a Christian while in the prison camp. In that prison camp, they tortured people who professed faith in Christ. I wish I had a copy of the message shared at church that day many years ago. I still remember his story to this day, and I am thankful for the impact this message has had on my life.

"And they overcame him by the blood of the Lamb <u>and by the word of their testimony</u>, and they did not love their lives to the death."
                                    – Revelation 12:11 (NKJV, emphasis added)

Get started with three FREE Life Story™ messages…

Everyone who has purchased this book will receive three Life Story downloads **free**. Just go to www.40DaystoFruitfulness.com[3] to download your three free Life Story messages. Additionally, you may know people personally who have great Life Story messages that you might be able to record and share with those who need to find Christ.

---

[3] Go to www.40DaysToFruitfulness.com to get your three free Life Story downloads.

Life Story Messages Include...

Joni Eareckson Tada (Famous speaker and artist) —
Joni was just an ordinary child growing up until a swimming accident left her forever paralyzed. Life as a quadriplegic has had challenges. Although Joni is now famous, you'll join her heart-gripping journey as she struggled to accept God's purposes after the accident. Her story is a powerful and encouraging testimony of God's desire for all things to work together for good and God's redeeming love even during tragedy.

Dave Dravecky (Famous baseball player) —
Millions know Dave Dravecky as the pitcher who battled his way back to the majors after cancer surgery. His left arm and shoulder were amputated after the cancer re-emerged. Discover how God strengthened both he and his wife during their valley of despair.

Can Science Prove There is a God? —
Discover the life story of a well-known scientist. This scientist is a lively and controversial scientist, even in many circles today. But, his life story will touch your heart, invigorate your mind, and encourage your faith. When he attempted to disprove the Bible scientifically, he was in for a big surprise. Great for intellectuals, teenagers, and everyone!

Astronaut General Charles Duke —
He was an astronaut on the moon, but his marriage was on the rocks. He had a problem! While his public life was soaring, his marriage was plummeting. Discover how Charles and his wife Dotty describe their quest for meaning and how they found meaning through life in Christ.

Application

What Life Story messages do you believe you should add to your toolbox? Ask God for wisdom in developing a collection of Life Story messages that you can give away for outreach. Perhaps the Lord will even use you to enhance (or start) your church's collection of Life Story messages. And, if you find or develop a great Life Story message, be sure to share it with others!

Daily Journal

What Life Story messages would you like to add to your outreach toolbox?

_____

_____

_____

_____

What opportunities have you had recently to share your faith?

_____

_____

_____

_____

Please write your prayer for today. Ask the Lord for wisdom in selecting Life Story testimony messages. Pray for opportunities to share these messages with others.

_____

_____

_____

_____

_____

Day #20 – Spiritual Strategies

 n the New Testament, a primary focus of Jesus' teaching was on heart issues. As you approach outreach and developing a lifestyle of fruitfulness, it is important to make sure that your heart and mind are aligned with Christ.

Power Thought for Today

Allow the Lord to transform your heart and mind to align with His will. When the Lord transforms your mind, you will see more of His will for your life. If there is sin in your life, repent and remove any sin in your life.

"Hide your face from my sins and blot out all my iniquity.
Create in me a pure heart, O God,
and renew a steadfast spirit within me.
Do not cast me from your presence or take your Holy Spirit from me.
Restore to me the joy of your salvation and grant me a willing spirit, to
*   sustain me.*
Then I will teach transgressors your ways, and sinners will turn back to
you."
                                    – Psalm 51:9-13 (NIV, Emphasis added)

Commitment

Heavenly Father,

I want to become better at sharing my faith. Please forgive me for not sharing my faith when I should have. There have been times when I have put my desires, my ambitions, and my fears above sharing the Gospel. Forgive me for not making the Great Commission the Greatest Commission of my life.

Father, show me anything in my heart that would hinder me in sharing the Gospel. Show me if I am holding anything against another. Help me to forgive as you have forgiven me.

Lord, I pray that You would give me opportunities to share with those who need to hear the Gospel over these 40 days and beyond. Father, help me to share the love of Christ with the type of people Christ shared with during his time on earth.

I ask that You would give me daily opportunities to reach out to people with the love of Christ. I pray that You would give me eyes to see, ears to hear, and a heart that cares. I pray for boldness and strength. Help me to help those who are touched by the Gospel to become committed disciples of Christ.

Father, I ask that You would help me to love people like You love people. I ask this in the Name of Jesus, Amen.

Date_____

Application

Ask the Lord to make your heart right before Him and to show you any issues you need to deal with in your life.

Pray, pray, pray…

1. Pray for opportunities to share the Gospel.
2. Pray for boldness.
3. Pray for God to guide you to people who need to hear about Christ.
4. Pray for creative ideas.
5. Pray for wisdom.

Daily Journal

Are there any heart issues that you need to deal with in your life? If so, write them down and your action plan for dealing with them.

_____

_____

_____

What opportunities have you had recently to share your faith?

_____

_____

_____

Please write your prayer for today. Pray and ask God to show you the things in your heart that you need to deal with. Ask that the Lord would help you to teach transgressors God's ways (Psalm 51:13).

_____

_____

_____

_____

_____

Day #21 – God's Hope in Times of Crisis

God often helps people and brings comfort during times of crisis. In reading the Scriptures, we know that times of crisis will come. There have been times of crisis throughout history, and it is only a matter of time before the next crisis emerges.

People also face personal crisis in families and communities. Whether a tragic death, an accident, a natural disaster, or violence, the people in your community will face a time of crisis at some point in their lives. Times of crisis lead to periods of fear and uncertainty where people need hope. During these times, you can help share God's hope by giving timely messages.

Power Thought for Today

Times of crisis reveal the foundations that people have been living their lives on. Foundations built on "sand" will shake during times of crisis. There are countless testimonies of people finding Christ and finding comfort and hope during times of crisis. You can help people find comfort and hope as you point them to the Savior.

"Therefore everyone who hears these words of mine and puts them into practice is like a wise man who built his house on the rock. The rain came down, the streams rose, and the winds blew and beat against that house; yet it did not fall, because it had its foundation on the rock. But everyone who hears these words of mine and does not put them into practice is like a foolish man who built his house on sand. The rain came down, the streams rose, and the winds blew and beat against that house, and it fell with a great crash."

– Matthew 7:24-27 (NIV)

Man finds Christ after an unthinkable tragedy at work...

Stuart and Deborah Hough, who live in Washington state, vividly remember a particular time when their pastor's sermons touched the lives of so many people who were hurting. A few years back, a former employee at Stuart's workplace came into the company, killed an employee, and committed suicide. "It really upset people at Stuart's job," recalled Deborah, "because this murder and suicide happed right there in one of the offices they all had to walk by and use."

For Stuart, it became a tremendous opportunity to take recorded messages from their church to his workplace. It was shortly after Easter and the pastor at Calvary Fellowship had just preached a wonderful Easter message that really explained the Gospel and the hope of the resurrection.

Stuart took a dozen or more messages to work following the incident. He recalled one gentleman, Steve, who was touched by the Easter message. "This (message) opened a door," stated Stuart. "Steve wanted to talk more. I took him to my Bible study group where he was able to get more answers to puzzling questions. During that time, he came to know the Lord as his personal Savior!" You can help people in times of crisis by giving them a word of encouragement and messages that explain the hope that is only found in Christ.

Application

Pray that the Lord would give you wisdom and show you how He can use you during times of crisis. Ask the Lord to help you prepare to reach the hurting during times of crisis. You may want to begin collecting resources that you can share with hurting people during times of crisis. Christ's message of hope can transform lives during times of crisis!

Daily Journal

Are there any people you know who are going through difficult times or times of crisis right now? If so, write down their names and pray for them. Ask God to help you to reach out to them.

_____

_____

_____

_____

What opportunities have you had recently to share your faith?

_____

_____

_____

_____

Please write your prayer for today. Ask God to help you to prepare to be ready to share God's hope during times of crisis.

_____

_____

_____

_____

_____

Day #22 – Messages for the Hurting

n the Gospels, Jesus touched and transformed the brokenhearted, sinners, and the oppressed. Tax collectors were turned into disciples. Fishermen were taught how to fish for souls. The thief on the cross was told he would be with Jesus in paradise.

You may not feel very equipped to reach every segment of your community. However, you can point them to Christ. By using CDs and recorded messages as tools, you can reach people that you might not otherwise be able to reach.

Power Thought for Today

Jesus reached out to people who were hurting and needy. He helped those who were sick and hungry. Jesus set an example that we should follow. As we reach out to the hurting, we are doing what Christ did while he was on the earth. The Lord touches and transforms our own hearts as we reach out to others with the love of Christ.

"Then the righteous will answer him, 'Lord, when did we see you hungry and feed you, or thirsty and give you something to drink? When did we see you a stranger and invite you in, or needing clothes and clothe you? When did we see you sick or in prison and go to visit you?'

"The King will reply, 'I tell you the truth, whatever you did for one of the least of these brothers of mine, you did for me.'"

– Matthew 25:37-40 (NIV)

Often the most compelling stories come from people who give messages to the hurting. One woman actually credits her physical healing to the encouragement the Lord gave her through audio messages. She had been in the hospital for two months fighting an illness that doctors feared would soon either kill her or leave her with brain damage. Visitors brought both teaching messages and music to her as gifts, which she listened to constantly. She gives God the credit and now testifies that *her complete recovery was the result of those recordings!*

Another Christian sent a special recorded message to a troubled friend who was addicted to drugs and alcohol. This friend heard the message and gave her life back to the Lord!

Woman struggling with the death of her husband touched by God!

A lady named Vicki was visiting her 90-year old grandmother, who lives in a nursing home. While there, she met Kathryn, a worker at the nursing home. Vicki started giving Kathryn messages on a regular basis. The Lord used these messages to create a bond between Kathryn and Vicki. One night Kathryn went home and found her husband dead at 42 years of age. After this event, Vicki was the first person that Kathryn called. Not long after that, Kathryn went to church with Vicki and gave her heart to the Lord. Now, she faithfully attends church. There has been a change in Kathryn's demeanor and whole life, even though she had to deal with her husband's tragic death. All of this change began with Vicki caring and sharing recorded messages with Kathryn.

A life-changing message touches a person struggling with suicide!

A church in Pennsylvania had a visitor come to their church. The church gave the visitor a copy of the message. The visitor insisted on paying for an extra copy of the message, even though the church offered the visitor an extra copy for free. Before too long, the visitor shared the message with someone they felt needed to hear the message. The person they gave the message to had been contemplating committing suicide. This person planned to end their own life. However, this person was so touched by the message that they didn't commit suicide! Instead, their life changed for the better through this message. When you give out a message, you never know the impact it may have on someone's life!

Man thinks of committing suicide before being sent to Iraq, but hears about God's love just in time!

A man who was about to be sent to Iraq saw a TV broadcast and requested a copy of an audio message called "Don't Quit, God Loves You". He had been thinking of killing himself before he came across this sermon. This was a just-in-time message! This man heard about God's love just-in-time!

Application

You may not feel very equipped to reach out to people in very difficult places who are hurting. Even if you have never gone through the situation yourself, you can pray for them, give messages of hope, and ask God to touch their lives. God may want to use you in ways you would never imagine, with people you would never expect.

Daily Journal

Write names the names of any people you know who are hurting or could use encouragement. List messages that you can share with people who are in need of encouragement.

_____

_____

_____

_____

What opportunities have you had recently to share your faith?

_____

_____

_____

_____

Please write your prayer for today. Ask God to help you reach out to the hurting, the brokenhearted, and those who need encouragement with the love of Christ.

_____

_____

_____

_____

_____

Day #23 – Messages on the Move

Take messages with you wherever you go. Men can put messages in a pocket or briefcase. Women often have the advantage of being able to carry several messages in their purse. I know of one lady who bought a special purse just so she could carry around a whole mini-army of messages!

You may be walking down the street, riding the subway, taking a cab, buying groceries, or standing in line waiting when you come across someone who could benefit from a message that you have with you.

I remember one time when a dog escaped and ran away from my house. A lady found the dog, saw the phone number on the dog tag, and called my house to let me know she had found the dog. When I went to pick up the dog, I offered her a message. She insisted that I did not need to give her a message as a thank you gift (people perceive messages as valuable!), but I believe she needed to hear the Gospel. She felt like she was just doing the right thing and did not need to receive a reward for it. A "lost" dog can even be helpful in reaching out to those around you. Take messages with you during your daily life and pray for opportunities to distribute the messages.

As you give out messages the impact of these messages may go on and on. The typical CD message is passed along to 3 or 4 people. Just imagine… every message you give out may be passed along to 3 or 4 people! Some CDs have even traveled across the country as they have been passed along to dozens of people.

> *The typical CD message is passed along to three or four people.*

Power Thought for Today

How many different places do you go where there are people? People are everywhere. People are at grocery stores. They are in checkout lines. They are walking down the street and in malls. People find people when they take walks, exercise, or go to sporting events. Just think… how many people did you cross paths with today or yesterday during your daily activities? Anywhere you go where people are meeting is an opportunity for outreach.

"Now then, we are ambassadors for Christ, as though God were pleading through us: we implore you on Christ's behalf, be reconciled to God. For He made Him who knew no sin to be sin for us, that we might become the righteousness of God in Him."
– II Corinthians 5:20-21 (NKJV)

Use CDs even at your house!

Pastor David Miller in Connecticut gave a man who fixed his furnace a recorded sermon message. The man thanked David not once but twice for the gift.

Shopping centers, malls, and hospitals!

A lady from a Baptist Church in Kentucky goes to shopping centers, malls, and hospitals on a regular basis with a bag full of sermon messages. She says that everyone always takes the messages! She prays, "Lord, point someone out to me who could use this (message)." Then, she walks up to people and tells them that the message will help them and that God wants them to have it. She has never had anyone reject a message. In fact, at times she has run out of messages and individuals have given her their name and address for her to mail them a message! People have joined her church as a result of her outreach.

Message leads to this former Muslim's miraculous healing and salvation!

"Thank God for my wonderful experience! I encountered Pastor Robinson, who preached Jesus to me. I did not want to hear him because I come from a Muslim family. He gave me a white cassette. Later that day, I started playing it...

I looked for [Pastor Robinson] the next day, with so many questions about Jesus. He answered them all, but I was not convinced. I went home and played the tape again. I have had poor eyesight since infancy, so I said 'if Jesus is missing from my life and He is Lord, then He must heal me.' I woke up the next day – and I could see clearly!

The doctor confirmed that I had no eye problem at all! I told my family, and they did not want to see me again. I know Jesus who heals will also care for me. Please pray for me." This man from Ghana, Africa is now following Jesus with all his heart.

A message left in a market helps this lady find Christ!

Someone left a message in a market that anyone could pick up and take with them. One day, a lady went into this market and picked up the message. The message was about "loving people" – an issue she struggled with. After listening to the message, she understood that God loved her, and she began going to church. She has experienced forgiveness and emotional healing as she continued attending church. Her life has turned around, and she is now serving the Lord!

Application

The Lord may want you to be the instrument that He uses to reach someone as you go along your way in your daily life. Ask the Lord to open your eyes to those around you who need to hear the Gospel. Look for opportunities in daily life. Be open to God's leading and be sensitive to the needs of others.

Daily Journal

Where are some of the places that you go regularly where you encounter other people?

_____

_____

_____

What opportunities have you had recently to share your faith?

_____

_____

_____

Please write your prayer for today. Ask God to help you to come across people during your daily life who need to hear the Gospel. Be prepared to share messages and your faith with others.

_____

_____

_____

_____

Day #24 – POWER DAY – Having a 'door to door' and 'house to house' impact

ecause there are people you do not know who live in your community, you may think that it would be difficult for you to have an impact on your community. However, it may be a lot less difficult than you think to reach these people!

Many people are helping their church to reach out to their entire community. They are reaching out to many people that they do not even know by leaving door hanger gift bags with CDs and an invitation to church on doorknobs in their community. Some churches also add a free gift such a light bulb or other small gift in addition to the CD.

This doorknob strategy is so easy and so powerful that children and youth are joining in this strategy too. It can be an exciting event for the entire family to go out into the community and do doorknob ministry.

Power Thought for Today

The early church went house to house to proclaim the good news of the Gospel. According to Acts chapter 5, the early church went to the temple courts daily and *from house to house*. They never stopped sharing the Gospel with others whether they were in the temple or going from house to house. The Lord may be in the process of mobilizing you so that you _never stop_ proclaiming the good news of the Gospel. In order to reach certain segments of your community, you will need to be on the move!

"<u>Day after day</u>, in the temple courts and <u>from house to house</u>, they <u>never stopped</u> teaching and proclaiming the <u>good news</u> that Jesus is the Christ."

– Acts 5:42 (NIV, emphasis added)

This woman had left her husband and was addicted to alcohol...

Gloria had left her husband, was rejected by her children, and had gotten enslaved to alcohol. She was without hope. A message was placed on Gloria's door on a Friday evening. The message was called "The Reality of Hell." She listened to the message on Saturday, went to church on Sunday, returned on Sunday night, and testified on Wednesday night how she had given her life to the Lord. Pastor Doug Foster says, "She said that from the moment she listened to the message left on her door, she has never had a desire to drink again! It's been about 4 years now, and she's never missed a service! If you met Gloria, you would have no idea what her life was like before she met Jesus!"

Today, Gloria serves on the toddler Sunday school team, sings in the choir, and just has a glow about her. She has such a good testimony at the construction company where she works, that the company donated both materials and labor for an entire section of the roof on the new church building. Not too long after this, she got up in church and thanked God that someone left a little audio sermon on her door one Friday night. God used that little message to transform her life!

Door to door messages... A message was 'broadcast' immediately!

A group of men from Immanuel Baptist Church in Kentucky went door to door handing out recorded messages. Before too long, they heard a loud sound. An elderly lady was sitting on her porch and when she got her copy, she immediately started listening to it loud enough that many could hear!

Door-to-door messages... Young people request the messages!

One evening several people from a church in the South were distributing messages. There was a group of young people outside a house that asked what they were doing. The young people said, "Wow! Can we have some of those?" The young people wanted the messages too!

Application

There are so many creative ways to reach out to your community with the good news of the Gospel. Ask the Lord to give you wisdom in identifying a 'door to door' or 'house to house' strategy to reach your community with the Gospel. It may be time to go on the move out into your community.

Daily Journal

What are some 'house to house' strategies that you could use to help reach your community? Which of these strategies will you implement and by when?

_____

_____

_____

What opportunities have you had recently to share your faith?

_____

_____

_____

Please write your prayer for today. Pray and ask the Lord to send you out into the harvest. Ask God to give you wisdom in regards to how to use 'door to door' and 'house to house' strategies to reach your community.

_____

_____

_____

_____

Day #25 – Get Creative

here are so many ways that you can reach out to others. You may meet someone today that the Lord wants you touch for His kingdom. Be creative. The Lord may have a special strategy that you can use to reach your community and those around you.

As you share your faith with others, be "generous" in sharing your faith. Sometimes, it may even take some creativity to generously share your faith.

Just imagine if you had a cure for cancer. Would you share this cure with as many people with cancer as possible? Some people might not even believe that you really had a cure for cancer – so you might need to get creative in sharing the cure. As believers, the Lord entrusts us with the spiritual cure for the spiritual diseases plaguing this world. It is our privilege and responsibility to share the spiritual cure with others. Seek to be someone who generously shares your faith with others.

Power Thought for Today

There may be a special or unique idea that is just right for impacting your community and those around you. Paul talks about how he became all things to all men so that by all means possible he might save some. It may take some creativity to reach people that you do not normally come in contact with in your daily life. Ask God to give you eyes to see and wisdom in reaching those around you.

"Though I am free and belong to no man, I make myself a slave to everyone, to win as many as possible. To the Jews I became like a Jew, to win the Jews. To those under the law I became like one under the law (though I myself am not under the law), so as to win those under the law. To those not having the law I became like one not having the law (though I am not free from God's law but am under Christ's law), so as to win those not having the law. To the weak I became weak, to win the weak. I have become all things to all men so that by all possible means I might save some. I do all this for the sake of the Gospel, that I may share in its blessings."

– I Corinthians 9:19-23 (NIV, emphasis added)

A unique car wash!

Joy of Faith Christian Center in Florida had a wonderful idea to hold a car wash to hand out free CDs. They posted a sign that read "Quality Car Wash $2." When a customer arrived, they washed the car, put Armor All® on the tires, cleaned the door jams, and put a car freshener inside the car. When they completed the job, the recipient would thank them and try to pay, but the church member would refuse the money saying, "We were going to give you $2 for letting us wash your car, but instead, we'd like to give you a $5 CD." The church members would not take any money, not even a tip. They just wanted to give, and they refused to accept any money. Their generosity caused several people to start crying, including one grown man. The people were touched because the volunteers did such an excellent job for free. Then the church members would say, "Hey, if you feel indebted to us, just come and visit us on Sunday." What a creative way to show God's love!

Movie theater outreach!

A small group of people decided to do a movie theater outreach after a movie with a Christian theme. One lady had already received the same message that was being handed out to those exiting the movie theater. She had received the audio and listened to the audio several days prior to the movie. When she saw the movie coupled with the audio she had just heard, she decided to commit her life to Christ. Then, only days after her powerful experience, she joined the outreach team. She helped the small group of people who were passing out the evangelistic message after the movie. The moviegoers were very appreciative to receive the audio messages. It only takes one family or a small group of people to do an outreach effort like this!

Over one hundred people saved, including many homeless people, in just three years!

A lady by the name of Dr. Golden felt led by God to give away inexpensive tape players to a large number of people, including many people who were poor or homeless. On a regular basis, she also gave them tapes. In her entire area, most of the homeless people came to Christ! In just 3 years, at least one hundred people were saved! These people told Dr. Golden that their salvation did not happen during the preaching at the church, and it did not happen when they were eating. Instead, it happened when they were sleeping under the bridge or when they were wandering in the woods, with their headphones on listening to the messages. Many people gave their hearts to Christ during these times. Over the course of three years, Dr. Golden saw many lives totally transformed by the power of Christ.

This man refused to go to church!

A man living on the East Coast, named Richard, had a friend who was terminally ill but did not want to go to church. For over a year, Richard got a copy of the sermon on CD each week and took it to his friend's house. Richard did not just give the man the messages. Instead, Richard drove around with his friend for 45 minutes each week so his friend could listen to the message. Eventually, Richard's friend said that he wanted to be saved. He made Jesus his Lord and Savior. Since that time, Richard's friend has gone to be home with the Lord. This man is now in glory because someone cared enough to creatively share the Gospel with him each week for over one year! 🕊

Application

Pray and ask the Lord to give you creative ideas for sharing your faith. Ask for creative ideas that will impact the lives of those around you and in your community.

Daily Journal

Write down ideas about how you might be able to share your faith with others in your community. Which of these ideas will you implement?

_____

_____

_____

What opportunities have you had recently to share your faith?

_____

_____

_____

Please write your prayer for today. Ask the Lord to help you to implement ideas that will touch the hearts of those in your community.

_____

_____

_____

_____

_____

Day #26 – Sending Messages

here are so many different ways that you can give messages to people. You can give messages as gifts, you can hand them to strangers, or you can even send them to people you know. Countless lives have been touched as people receive messages as a gift from someone who knows or cares about them.

Earlier in the book, there was a story about a little girl who wanted her father to come to know Jesus. This little girl played an important role in her father's salvation by mailing him copies of her pastor's sermons, even though he lived in another state.

You may have friends or relatives that live a good distance away. You may be able to impact their lives for eternity by sending message to these friends or relatives.

Power Thought for Today

People love to go to their mailbox and receive personal mail. Mail from a friend or relative is normally received as a gift. Friends and family tend to be very appreciative of receiving mail. You may be able to touch the lives of friends and family by sending them sermons and special messages.

Think through your friends, family members, and acquaintances. Is their anyone you believe that the Lord wants you like to touch by sending messages to them?

Just imagine the joy in heaven that would come from the salvation of your unsaved friends and family. Be persistent in reaching out to those you care about.

"Or suppose a woman has ten silver coins and loses one. Does she not light a lamp, sweep the house and search carefully until she finds it? And when she finds it, she calls her friends and neighbors together and says, 'Rejoice with me; I have found my lost coin.' In the same way, I tell you, there is rejoicing in the presence of the angels of God over one sinner who repents."

– Luke 15:8-10 (NIV)

Family reunited thanks to a cassette!

Pastor Larry Parks in Florida shared how a family was reconciled due to the message ministry. The gentleman in charge of the message ministry had been estranged from his older children for about ten years. The man started sending his children messages every week. "Then one Wednesday night at service, this man's family showed up at church, completely to his surprise. His family had taken the name and address (printed on the message), and then they drove from New York to Florida to surprise their dad." Because of those messages, this family was reunited after ten years!

Friends saved...

Many people share CDs with their friends. Kenny in Westville, Oklahoma, sends sermons to his friends. "Many have been saved," he reports, "because I was persistent in feeding them with God's Word!"

Application

Ask the Lord to bring people to your mind that you should call on the phone or send a message. Even when people move or live a distance from you, you can still have an impact on their lives. Perhaps, there is even someone that you should send messages to regularly.

Write down the names of friends, family members, and acquaintances who live a good distance away from you and need to hear the good news of the Gospel. Perhaps some have moved, gone away to college, or joined the military. Chances are, you'll be able to think of quite a few. Which of these people will you start sharing messages with on a regular basis?

_____

_____

_____

What opportunities have you had recently to share your faith?

_____

_____

_____

Please write your prayer for today. Ask the Lord to give you creative ideas to touch the lives of those you know. Give messages regularly to those God places on heart.

_____

_____

_____

_____

Day #27 – Places You Never Take Messages

When you give a CD or recorded message to someone, the message will frequently get passed on and on. CDs can easily be passed along to three or four people... or more! CDs and recorded messages end up in places you never take them.

Even lost messages have led people to Christ. When you give a CD to someone, you never know where the message may eventually end up or whose life the message may end up touching. Passed along messages are touching the lives of countless people.

Power Thought for Today

CDs and recorded messages have ended up traveling across countless miles and states as they are passed from person to person. When you give away a message, you don't know how many people God may touch through that one message.

The CDs and messages you give away may have a far-reaching impact on people you do not even know. Some single CDs or tapes have led to the salvation of ten or more people as one message has been passed along from person to person. The Lord saves those who come to him, whether near or far.

"Therefore he is able to save completely those who come to God through him (Jesus), because he always lives to intercede for them."
– Hebrews 7:25 (NIV)

> *The typical CD message is passed along to 3 or 4 people. When you give away a message, you never know where or with whom God may use it!*

Even a lost message can reach people for Christ!

A man at Port Gibson, Mississippi was at the town landfill and noticed a recorded message that had been thrown away. (Or perhaps it had fallen out of someone's pocket or gotten lost. Messages don't get thrown away very often, because CDs and recorded messages are valuable.) The message looked professionally printed, so the man picked it up. It was a message from a pastor at a local church. The message seemed to be in good condition, so he took it home and listened to it. He enjoyed the message so much that he visited the church, made Jesus the Lord of his life, and became a member of that church.

God can use even a discarded or lost CD to touch a life for eternity. You never know where the CDs you give out may end up. But before anyone can receive your CD "out in the world," someone in your church must "take the message" with them out into the world.

Message left in rental car leads to salvation!

A message preached by a pastor in Missouri was left in a rental car. A man rented this rental car with the message that was left behind. This man's curiosity about the message stirred him to listen to the message. As a result of listening to this message, this man committed his life to Christ. He then took this message that he found in the rental car home to his family. This man's family listened to the message, and they too were led to salvation through this message.

A maintenance man finds a message and decides to follow Jesus!

A maintenance man, Nolan, was at work doing his regular duties when he came across a message that had been left behind. The title of the message grabbed his attention, so he decided to take it home and listen to it. Nolan committed his life to the Lord as a direct result of listening to the message. Before long, Nolan and his wife began worshipping the Lord together at church. Three of his grown daughters and their families also started living for the Lord because of that message. These four families have now been faithful to God and attending church for several years. Pastor Eakins, a minister who has seen the Lord do marvelous things as the Word of God has gone out through messages shares this story often. Pastor Eakins says that when someone asks if distributing so many messages produces excessive waste, he always recounts this glorious story.

Messages found in a Goodwill store help a lady to find a church home!

God can use messages anywhere. Marilyn Lawson in California shared how a lady found a recorded message at a Goodwill store. "There's a lady in our church who came and joined after hearing one of the pastor's messages that she found at a Goodwill store!" Marilyn says that God can use every message you make! Marilyn encourages everyone to get more messages out. ❧

Application

Pray and ask the Lord that the CDs and messages you give out would be passed along to people who need to hear the Gospel. Ask God that the messages given out would touch many lives for eternity. Pray that the Lord would use these messages in many different places to touch lives.

Daily Journal

Write down any new ideas you have in how you can get messages out to people who need to hear them.

_____

_____

_____

_____

What opportunities have you had recently to share your faith?

_____

_____

_____

Please write your prayer for today. Ask the Lord to cause the people you give messages to pass them along to others who need to hear that message. Pray that the messages would have an eternal impact for God's kingdom.

_____

_____

_____

_____

Day #28 – The Impact May Go On and On

When a sermon or special message goes outside the four walls of the church, the impact of that message can go on and on. The CD or other recorded message may touch the life of someone right now. Or, the message may touch the life of someone a year from now or even many, many years from now.

The impact of the CDs and messages you give away may go on for a long time. It is amazing how messages preached 10, 15, or even 20 years ago can have an impact on someone's life today.

Power Thought for Today

The CDs and recorded messages you give out can be "messengers" spreading the good news. Although you may not be gifted as an evangelist, you can do the work of an evangelist by taking messages preached from the pulpit out into the community. And, you never know how long a particular message may have an impact in your community and beyond. People have been saved decades after they first received a recorded message!

"How, then, can they call on the one they have not believed in? And how can they believe in the one of whom they have not heard? And how can they hear without someone preaching to them? And how can they preach unless they are sent? As it is written,

'How beautiful are the feet of those who bring good news!'"
– Romans 10:14-15 (NIV)

Man takes 20 year-old tape out of a box and gets saved!

"It might be months or years down the road that somebody will finally listen" to a message they have received. "But they will listen to it," says Pastor Ray Witherington in South Carolina. Messages rarely get thrown in the garbage.

"I gave one of my message tapes to my sister over 20 years ago," Pastor Ray continued. "It was a tape dealing with being saved. She was married at the time, and neither she nor her husband were Christians. My sister put that tape in a box."

"Over the process of time, my sister and her husband, Glen, were divorced. Several years after the divorce and 20 years after I gave it to my sister, Glen was looking through boxes and found that tape. He listened to that tape. The spirit of God touched his heart, and he gave his life to Jesus Christ. He wrote to my mother about what happened, who in turn relayed the story to me."

"I gave Glen a call," shared Pastor Ray. He was so excited to hear from me. We prayed over the phone. Glen shared that he was going to go on (serving) the Lord!

He also shared that the tape he found – that had been in a box for 20 years – was what really helped him." That is the power of giving messages away. The Lord can use them now or at anytime in the future.

Forgotten message preached in the U.S. leads to a Jewish man finding His Messiah in Bethlehem!

Several years ago, Pastor Robert Rivers and Salem Baptist Church had enjoyed a visit from a young newspaperman from Jerusalem, who reported on many things concerning Christians there. Pastor Rivers preached on the power of God's Holy Spirit to reveal truth to the Jews during this newspaperman's visit.

Fast forward several years later to Christmas Eve, when the pastor's telephone rang late at night. "The phone call woke me up in the middle of the night," he recalled. The phone call was from a Jewish man who had just listened to the message preached several years earlier. The Jewish man had just accepted Christ as his Messiah. "And, he was so excited about it, he had completely forgotten there was a huge time difference between us."

The man was calling with his salvation report – from Bethlehem – on Christmas Eve!

Tape given to man when he was 10 years old changes his life in his twenties!

A while back, a church got a call from a young man who attended services when he was 10 years old and was now in his twenties. Children tend to hold onto messages and consider them prized possessions. This young man took home a tape when he was 10 years old and put it away.

Over the next few years, like many teenagers, he got into trouble, became rebellious, got involved with drugs and alcohol, and did a lot of terrible things. His life had become a complete mess.

One day, when the man was in his early twenties, he was going through some items and came across the message he had received when he was 10 years old. He listened to the message, the Lord touched his heart, and he came back to God.

The young man started regularly contacting the church he had attended when he was 10 years old. He talks to the pastor quite frequently, and he is now free from drugs and alcohol. The Lord has put it on this young man's heart to minister and preach the Word of God. He now shares his testimony with boys at a local rehabilitation center. ⁀

Application

Pray and ask the Lord that the CDs and messages you give out would touch people at just the right point in time in their lives. Pray that the impact of these messages would go on and on for many years.

Daily Journal

Today's Date_____

Write down the names of people that you might be able to give messages.

_____

_____

_____

_____

What opportunities have you had recently to share your faith?

_____

_____

_____

Please write your prayer for today. Pray and ask God to use the messages you give out at just the right time. Pray that these messages would impact lives, even if the impact is many years away.

_____

_____

_____

_____

_____

Day #29 – Business Owners and Managers

In the New Testament, the early Christians reached out to business people as a regular part of daily life. One the converts, Lydia, was a buyer and seller of cloth. Today, dealing with people in business is still a regular part of daily life. Some of these people are small business owners who own shops and restaurants, while others are employed by businesses.

When you meet an owner of a business, one of the things you can do is to let them know that you are going to pray for their business and ask God to bless them. This simple act of kindness has touched many business owners.

Power Thought for Today

As you go through daily life, be aware of the people you are encountering along your journey. Many of these people will be employees or owners of small businesses such as restaurants and shops. Be prepared to share the Gospel with those you meet during daily life.

'"On the Sabbath we (Paul and his traveling companions) went outside the city gate to the river, where we expected to find a place of prayer. We sat down and began to speak to the women who had gathered there. One of those listening was a woman named Lydia, a dealer in purple cloth from the city of Thyatira, who was a worshiper of God. The Lord opened her heart to respond to Paul's message. When she and the members of her household were baptized, she invited us to her home. 'If you consider me a believer in the Lord,' she said, 'come and stay at my house.' And she persuaded us."
— Acts 16:13-15 (NIV)

Successful businessman saved through recorded message!

Bryan was a successful businessman in the construction field. He heard an evangelistic recorded message that changed his life. Bryan says, "It made me turn…and I fell in love with the Lord."

Almost immediately, Bryan started witnessing using…you guessed it… recorded messages. He now uses CDs to reach the lost regularly! He knows these messages will change others, and he has seen many lives changed. He has a real burden to reach as many people as he can, and he does it through recorded messages.

God was not done changing things for Bryan's family. Soon the whole family was saved. God called Bryan to leave his successful business and change the direction of his life. He now pastors a small but growing church in Arizona. Just one little message changed the course Bryan's life, and now Bryan is impacting the lives of countless others.

Store owners and managers play recorded sermons!

Pastor Larry Parks from Florida shared "One of our members walked into a local grocery story," Pastor Larry recalled. "This person was surprised when they heard a familiar sermon being played in the produce section. It turns out that another member had given the Produce Manager a copy of that week's message." Reaching people we come in contact with every day through messages is such a tremendous and easy strategy for evangelism!

Pastor Larry had another similar testimony he shared, "Somebody from our congregation had given a message to the owner of a local restaurant, and the owner was Hindu. Another one of our members walked into that restaurant later that week and heard the message being played again." "It's having quite an evangelistic effect on our community. People are being reached for Christ through our (message) ministry."

Application

Ask God to help you to be more aware of opportunities to share the Gospel with those you meet. Many of these people will be connected with businesses and some will be owners of small businesses. Develop strategies for reaching those around you.

Daily Journal

List businesses, small shops, and restaurants that you visit frequently. Think of ways to reach people at the places you go frequently.

_____

_____

_____

What opportunities have you had recently to share your faith?

_____

_____

_____

Please write your prayer for today. Pray and ask God to help you to reach business owners, those in business, and those you meet in daily life.

_____

_____

_____

_____

Day #30 – POWER DAY - Developing a Personal Outreach Site

Power Days: On power days, you will learn how to extend and multiply your impact. Power Days will show you how to increase your outreach impact in your community, how you can help your church multiply its effectiveness, or how to multiply your own personal outreach efforts.

Just as carrying various formats of recorded messages can help you reach more people, combining other technologies will also increase your impact in sharing the Gospel. As you combine technologies, you will be adding more tools to your outreach toolbox. More tools will give you more opportunities and more ways to share the good news with others.

You can combine recorded physical media such as CDs and DVDs with an MP3 strategy. For instance, you can give out CDs that have a website address on them. Additional messages can posted on the website that people can listen to or download to an MP3 player. The website can be your church's website. Or, you can develop your own personal outreach site with messages that are meaningful to you and would be of interest to someone wanting to learn more about God.

Another strategy that you can use is to add messages or message links on any personal web pages that you already have. With all the social websites (Myspace, Facebook, etc.), this is a great way to share the Gospel with others.

If you decide to post messages online or create your own personal website that contains outreach messages, you will need to find messages where the copyright allows you to post the messages online. In posting messages online, it is important to find high-powered messages and testimonies.

On the website associated with this book, there are resource links to a library of messages that you can use for outreach on CD or post online without violating copyrights. There is also a collection of evangelistic "Life Story" messages from famous athletes, astronauts, scientists, and others that can really grow your collection of outreach messages. You can add these to your church's website or create your own outreach website within a few hours. To find resource links for these messages, go to www.40DaysToFruitfulness.com. ᕙᕗ

Power Thought for Today

By this time, you may be in the process of becoming more activated in outreach than you would have ever imagined. You can begin to think through other ways to increase your impact in reaching the lost. For instance, should you have your own personal outreach website or use pages on a social networking website for outreach? You may be able to take the Gospel to remote places right from your own computer.

"He said to them, 'Go into all the world and preach the good news to all creation. Whoever believes and is baptized will be saved, but whoever does not believe will be condemned.'" – Mark 16:15-16 (NIV)

"How beautiful on the mountains
are the feet of those who bring good news,
who proclaim peace,
who bring good tidings,
who proclaim salvation,
who say to Zion,
'Your God reigns!'"
                                            – Isaiah 52:7 (NIV)

Application

Make a decision to share the Gospel through every opportunity that God gives you. In order to be ready for the people that the Lord brings across your path, you may need to prepare for these opportunities in advance. Pray for God's wisdom in preparing for these opportunities or in creating these opportunities. There may be a special idea that is just the right idea for impacting those around you. Or, the Lord may give you opportunities to touch those around the world through the Internet.

Daily Journal

How can you use the Internet in sharing the Gospel? How can you combine Internet strategies with giving away CDs? Activate the ideas that the Lord lays on your heart.

_____

_____

_____

What opportunities have you had recently to share your faith?

_____

_____

_____

Please write your prayer for today. Ask the Lord to give you wisdom in preparing for opportunities to share the Gospel and in advancing God's kingdom by using the Internet.

_____

_____

_____

_____

_____

Day #31 – GIVE, GIVE, GIVE

t's amazing how you can share the good news of the Gospel in so many ways with others. It is important to become a generous person in sharing your faith. Allow the Gospel to overflow from the generosity of your heart. The Lord has given each believer a wellspring of life through the power of the Gospel.

"A generous man will prosper; he who refreshes others will himself be refreshed." – Proverbs 11:25 (NIV)

In thinking about being generous in sharing the Gospel, it is important to remember that the Gospel really is good news! Without the life-changing truths of the Gospel, many of the people you know and meet are in for some really bad news.

Just imagine if you started to pass out stacks of $100 bills on the street. What would happen? Now, imagine that you went back to the same place day after day and passed out $100 bills? Soon this unusual behavior would cause floods of people to come. This activity would draw crowds of people, and it would be featured in newspapers and on the news. The real truth is that you have something that is much more valuable than even stacks of $100 bills. The Gospel has an eternal value that is not measurable by money.

Power Thought for Today

If your friends or family were visiting you and were thirsty, would you offer them a glass of refreshing water? Of course! In the same way, the world without the Gospel is thirsting for spiritual truth. The world needs a drink from the life-giving water of Jesus.

Ask the Lord to help you overcome the fears and other things that hold you back in sharing your faith. Become generous in sharing your faith and what God has done in your life.

"For what profit is it to a man if he gains the whole world, and loses his own soul? Or what will a man give in exchange for his soul?"
– Matthew 16:26 (NKJV)

129

Thrift Stores

At a church in South Carolina, several members in the congregation put messages in thrift stores. They copy the messages, nicely package them, put them in bags with other gift items, and donate them to local thrift stores. The thrift stores put the bags on the shelves, and they are normally gone in two days!

The thrift store makes a little money and the messages go out to people they might never come in contact with or ever even know. It is a double blessing.

The church is also seeing fruit from this ministry. For instance, the church received a call from a man named Thomas, and he received a message through one of the thrift stores. Soon, he visited the church along with his wife and daughter. The Lord is using the thrift store packages to touch lives!

Truckers are coming to Christ all across the country and beyond!

Several truck drivers distribute 4,000 recorded messages a month all over the United States from just one church! This one church is having a big impact well-beyond its local community. These truck drivers regularly use fishbowls to distribute these messages to other truck drivers. On many occasions, these messages have touched truck drivers' lives for eternity. Some truck drivers who have listened to these messages have even turned their lives to Christ and become preachers. One truck driver gave his life to Christ while listening to these messages on the road. Then, he became a truck driver serving the military in Iraq. To keep serving God while in Iraq, he distributes messages to troops all over Iraq. This man, a truck driver, has been able to be a missionary while on the road and around the world!

Shy people!

At Immanuel Baptist Church in Kentucky, individuals that are very shy about talking to someone about salvation are going out and just hanging recorded messages on people's doors. People are joining the church through this strategy!

Man puts messages in with orders

A man uses his business to reach people for Christ. He makes a lot of sales to businesses all over the country. Some of his customers are construction firms with 200 to 300 employees. He places a few messages in the box with orders. He does not even tell them that he is sending the messages; he just believes that those who need to hear the messages will receive them!

Each message is prayed over before he sends it. It does take time for him to pray over the messages, but he enjoys it. He often prays, "Father, I send forth the Word of God, and as it's written, I know it won't come back void. I pray that You would put it in the hand that needs to hear the message of God. I pray that it will be a blessing to whoever hears."

This man believes that the Lord does the drawing from these messages. He feels he is responsible to plant the seeds and allow God to do the work from there.

130

Application

God has given each believer something good – the good news of the Gospel. This goodness from the Lord needs to be shared with others. Whatever your life situation, there are special ways that you can be generous in sharing your faith. Whether it be at a daycare, packaging messages for thrift stores, or distributing messages in your community, you can become generous in sharing with others.

Daily Journal

Today's Date_____

What are some ways that you can be generous in sharing your faith with others?

_____

_____

_____

_____

What opportunities have you had recently to share your faith?

_____

_____

_____

Please write your prayer for today. Ask the Lord to help you be generous in sharing your faith with others. Ask the Lord for wisdom in ways and places you can share your faith.

_____

_____

_____

_____

Day #32 – Special Messages

 aving special audio messages for people in specific situations can multiply your outreach opportunities. Just imagine the impact of giving someone just the right message at just the right time.

When people are dealing with specific situations, they are often very receptive to a message that deals with their situation. Friends are often blessed when we care enough to give them a message that deals with exactly what they are going through right at that moment.

You can assemble a toolbox that equips you with messages that you can give to people in specific life situations. Then, you can give away the right message at the right time when you encounter people in specific life situations.

For instance, you can have messages to give to people when they are dealing with difficulties in raising their children, problems in their marriage, sickness, addictions, stress, or grieving the loss of a loved one.

Power Thought for Today

A timely word can touch the soul! When you share words of wisdom with someone at just the right time it will bless their heart and yours as well.

You may give someone a timely message that saves a soul, saves a marriage, or helps someone at a critical or even devastating point in their life.

"A man finds joy in giving an apt reply —
and how good is a timely word!" – Proverbs 15:23 (NIV)

Special messages – living single, etc.

Annette Flowers shares the pastoral duties at Church at Liberty with her husband Michael. Annette has many stories of people who were touched by receiving one of her messages… "Quite some time ago, I did a message on living single," Annette shared. "There was a lady who was a new believer that was struggling with her singleness. At the time, this person was not attending services at our church, but a lady from our congregation shared the message about living single with this woman. After hearing the message, this lady decided to make a change in her lifestyle and completely commit her life to the Lord. Here is a lady that was blessed by one of my messages, and she wasn't even present at the time I spoke it." This lady's life changed, because someone gave her a recorded message!

Marriage helped just in time!

There was a young man whose marriage was in trouble. He and his wife were struggling. He received a message entitled 'The Role of a Christian Husband' by an evangelist. Through this message the man was blessed and encouraged. He listened to this message at just the right time, because his marriage had been in trouble. He is very grateful that he received this message at just the right time.

Application

There are so many different life situations that we encounter with those around us. Ask the Lord to help you develop a collection of resources for the needs of those around you. And pray that the Lord would give you wisdom in what to say and when to give messages and resources to those who need a timely word. Ask the Lord to help you give messages to people in season.

Ask the Lord to help you give
messages to people in season.

Daily Journal Today's Date_____

What are some of the types of messages (for specific life situations) that you would like to have in your toolbox to give to those who come across your path?

_____

_____

_____

What opportunities have you had recently to share your faith?

_____

_____

_____

_____

Please write your prayer for today. Ask the Lord to help you in developing the right collection of resources (CDs, books, DVDs, etc.) to share. Start to assemble the collection of tools that you need. You may even be able to help your church in assembling this toolbox as well.

_____

_____

_____

_____

Day #33 – Sharing With Your Mouth

 ver the past several weeks, you have been learning how to share CDs and recorded messages. CDs and recorded messages are some of the easiest and most effective tools for sharing the Gospel. As you share CDs and messages with others, you will find yourself having greater boldness for sharing the Gospel with your "mouth" and in other ways.

Allow the Lord to grow your abilities and your effectiveness in sharing the Gospel in multiple ways. Work on being as effective as you can be in sharing CDs and recorded messages for outreach. Next, work on being as effective as you can be in sharing the Gospel with your mouth while still continuing to give out CDs and recorded messages. Then, combine sharing verbally with giving people a message at the end of the conversation, even if the conversation is brief.

In thinking about people who can talk to just about anyone about the Gospel, one person that I know very well comes to mind. It seems like my father, Johnny Berguson, can get into a conversation with anyone, just about anywhere about Christ! He is an evangelist. He carries CDs so that these conversations he has started can have a greater impact when the conversation is over.

CDs and recorded messages can be a great supplement to conversations where you are sharing the Gospel, or they may help open the door to sharing the Gospel. As you grow in your faith and in reaching out to others, you will develop more and more ways to combine tools to reach those who do not yet know Christ. The Lord can help you develop a lifestyle of fruitfulness as you learn when to use different tools to reach out to others.

Power Thought for Today

Your mouth has the power to build up and the power to tear down. Even small conversations can have a lasting impact. Ask the Lord to cause your mouth to overflow with the good news of the Gospel.

Choose to lay down your life for others by sharing the Gospel with those you meet!

"This is how we know what love is: Jesus Christ laid down his life for us. And we ought to lay down our lives for our brothers."

– 1 John 3:16 (NIV)

"For we must all appear before the judgment seat of Christ, that each one may receive what is due him for the things done while in the body, whether good or bad. Since, then, we know what it is to fear the Lord, we try to persuade men. What we are is plain to God, and I hope it is also

Power Thought for Today (continued)

plain to your conscience."

　　　　　　　　　　　　　　　　　– II Corinthians 5:10-11 (NIV, emphasis added)

Man finds Christ and helps many of his students find Christ as well!

Mike was an instructor who taught Eastern meditation and yoga. He started to have some questions about God. A man who had previously been into Eastern meditation himself talked to Mike about Christ. Because of the man's background, he was able to talk to Mike in a way he could understand. Mike accepted Christ as His Lord and Savior. He told his students that although he had not intended to, he had been leading them away from truth. Many of his top students put their faith in Christ.

Lady finds Christ after the Gospel and baptism are explained to her...

A lady named Tasha was not a Christian, but she started attending a Bible study. After she had been attending the Bible study for several weeks, there was a night when no one showed up to the Bible study, except for Tasha and a friend that Tasha had brought along with her. The Bible study leader took the evening to explain sin, Jesus' atonement, salvation, and baptism. That was the night that Tasha decided to give her life to Christ. And, she was baptized a few weeks later! Tasha's new friends helped her to find faith in Christ and make changes in her life for the better. Tasha is grateful for her new life in Christ!

Greg didn't even like Christians... but these Christians answered his questions...

Greg disliked Christians. He thought they were just a bunch of hypocrites. Then, he met some Christians who would soon become his friends. He could tell that they were really trying to follow Christ wholeheartedly. They started answering Greg's questions about Christ. Then, one of Greg's new friends started to share how God was answering his prayers. After this, Greg's heart was touched, and he chose to follow Christ. ☙

Application

Ask the Lord to help you grow in the ways you are sharing your faith. As you share messages, you will start to share your faith with more people through your mouth. When you open up and share stories about how Christ has worked in practical ways in your life, people will be able to see Christ moving in your life.

Daily Journal

How do you think you can combine sharing your faith with your mouth and recorded messages, or are you already doing this?

_____

_____

_____

_____

What opportunities have you had recently to share your faith?

_____

_____

_____

_____

Please write your prayer for today. Ask the Lord to help you to open your mouth and share the Gospel with boldness. Pray that the Lord will increase your fruitfulness for His kingdom.

_____

_____

_____

_____

_____

Day #34 – The Power of a Message in God's Hands

Too often when we think of reaching out to others, we look first at our own abilities. It is too easy to get focused on own abilities, instead of the power of the message of the good news – the Gospel. The Gospel has the power to change lives, art, music, culture, and even entire nations.

If you had a stick of dynamite in your hand, would you be focused on the strength of your body or your own abilities? No! You would be focused on the power of the stick of dynamite.

The power of the Gospel is stronger than any stick of dynamite! It is more powerful than an atomic bomb! A stick of dynamite and an atomic bomb have power to destroy, whereas, the power of the Gospel has the life-giving power to restore and transform. Essentially, the Gospel does the opposite of a stick of dynamite or a bomb. The Gospel takes things that are all messed up, transforms them, and restores lives. Just think about the life-giving power of the Gospel to restore and transform!

Just like a stick of dynamite must be ignited in order to detonate, the Gospel must be ignited. In order for the Gospel to be "ignited or spiritually detonated," people must first "hear" the Gospel. Romans 10:17 says that faith comes by hearing and hearing by the word of God. But, how is the Gospel ignited in the hearts of men and women? What ignites the power of the Gospel? From the Scripture, is it clear that the Holy Spirit is the "igniter" of the Gospel in the hearts and minds of men and women.

This analogy is really meant to illustrate that you should not be focused on your own power and abilities (or limitations) as you share the Gospel. Instead, you need to focus on God's power. It is important to pray that God's power is released in the hearts and minds of men. You simply need to be a vessel that God can use to work through.

Power Thought for Today

When we speak words or give out messages, the Lord can ignite these words with power to transform hearts and lives. When we share CDs, it can be like sending little missionaries all over the world.

> *CDs and messages are like little missionaries in God's hands!*

"As the rain and the snow come down from heaven, and do not return to it without watering the earth and making it bud and flourish, so that it yields seed for the sower and bread for the eater, so is my word that goes out from my mouth: It will not return to me empty, but will accomplish what I desire and achieve the purpose for which I sent it."

– Isaiah 55:10-11 (NIV)

Dad not convinced...

A Christian father was not convinced of the value of giving away messages. The father did not know if it was a good use of money. Then, his adult son, Jimmy, gave a message to the mail carrier that would change her life. The mail carrier listened to the message, and it touched her heart deeply.

The mail carrier talked to Jimmy's father about the message. Actually, she went on and on about the message.

Then, the mail carrier asked Jimmy's dad who the gentleman was that had given her the message. She said, "I've never heard a message like that before!"

In good humor he responded, "That was no gentleman. That was my son!" The mail carrier continued, "I've never heard a recording that spoke to me so much. It has changed my life!"

Now, Jimmy's dad is excited about the power of messages. He now gives out messages regularly including copies of the same message that impacted the mail carrier!

Police officer finds Christ while in his squad car!

A police officer sat right in his squad car and listened to a recorded message. Right there in his car, he gave his life to Christ. This police officer was transformed from being a person with no interest in the things of the Lord to a person who now trusts the Lord sincerely. Eleven years later, this police officer is still a faithful member of his church along with his family. He regularly shares his faith with other police officers and with groups of young people.

The value of a message in God's hands!

Pastor Steve Boyer of Christ Community Church shared at a Media Ministry conference "who" is responsible for the success of the life-changing impact of messages. "It depends," he said, "on whose hands it's in. In my hands, a basketball is worth about nineteen dollars. In Michael Jordan's hands, that same basketball is worth thirty-three million dollars. In my hands, this [message] isn't worth too much. But in God's hands, a message ministry is like the loaves and fish that were blessed and increased to feed a multitude." Pastor Steve Boyer's church quickly grew from 700 to over 2,200 people after launching and promoting a Messages-To-Go ministry several years ago.

Application

Ask the Lord to help you to see the power of the good news when the Lord uses the good news of the Gospel to touch lives. Pray that the Lord would help you to share the Gospel. Think through new ways or new places you might be able to share the Gospel with others. Continue to ask the Lord for greater fruitfulness and boldness in your life.

Daily Journal

If you had no fear, how and where would you share the Gospel? What are some ways you can focus on God's power instead of your own abilities? Have you ever been held back in sharing your faith because you were focused on your own abilities? Explain.

_____

_____

_____

_____

What opportunities have you had recently to share your faith?

_____

_____

_____

Please write your prayer for today. Ask the Lord to help you to share the Gospel with boldness both with your mouth and through recorded messages. Pray and ask the Lord to energize your heart for outreach and to activate you into greater fruitfulness.

_____

_____

_____

_____

Day #35 - Grow, **Grow, GROW**

A contagious Christian is a growing Christian. You are either growing in your Christian faith or you're not growing. There is no middle ground! The importance of ongoing spiritual growth is vital to developing a lifestyle of fruitfulness.

When God's Word is impacting your own heart and life, you are seeing God work in your life. This growth is often contagious. And, no matter how much you grow in your faith, you will still have room to grow. Even the Apostle Paul kept growing and growing!

Many believers who see increased effectiveness in outreach are growing as they listen to their pastor's sermon again during the week. It is so easy to get a copy of the sermon and listen to it again during the week. This helps in two areas. First, you cannot apply what you do not remember. Many times, pastors spend 10, 15, or more hours preparing for the sermon. The weekly sermon is a valuable tool for your own spiritual growth, not just outreach. When you listen to the sermon again during the week, this helps you both remember and apply the sermon. Second, it also makes it even easier to give out sermon messages when you are excited, because you are listening to the messages and applying them in your own life. You will remember more, and you will have more to talk about when you meet people during your daily activities.

You will find many messages even more powerful the second time that you listen to them. You will pick up things that you did not catch the first time you listened to the message. Sometimes, you may feel that you did not get a lot from a message when you listened to it the first time, compared to how much you get out of the message when you listened to it a second time.

Power Thought for Today

One of the most powerful evangelistic forces in the world is a group of excited, enthusiastic, and growing Christians. As you develop more spiritual growth habits and develop your abilities in sharing your faith, you can join this evangelistic force in powerfully advancing God's kingdom!

"Not that I (Paul) have already obtained all this, or have already been made perfect, but I press on to take hold of that for which Christ Jesus took hold of me. Brothers, I do not consider myself yet to have taken hold of it. But one thing I do: Forgetting what is behind and straining toward what is ahead, I press on toward the goal to win the prize for which God has called me heavenward in Christ Jesus.

All of us who are mature should take such a view of things. And if on some point you think differently, that too God will make clear to you."

– Philippians 3:12-15 (NIV)

"But the seed on good soil stands for those with a noble and good heart, who hear the word, <u>retain it</u>, and by persevering produce a crop."

– Luke 8:15 (NIV, emphasis added)

Keep growing spiritually as you listen to the message again!

A while back, Zarlene Thomas of Calvary Revival Church shared about the importance of listening to messages again and again. "How are people going to grow spiritually unless they can hear and apply the Word, if they can't remember what was preached? We all need to listen to the sermons again! My pastor often jokingly says from the pulpit that we need to hear each message about 48 times to make it stick. He is always encouraging our church to get the message out. Our church is growing and the lives of people are changing as a result!"

Ex-con's life transformed as he keeps listening to sermons again and again!

If you make a commitment to listen to your pastor's sermons again and again, this spiritual discipline will grow your faith no matter who you are. One ex-con got saved and started constantly listening to sermons. He would meet with his pastor regularly, and he kept listening and listening to sermons. When he had questions, he would ask his pastor about these questions. As he kept listening, this man's heart, mind, and will were transformed into the image of Christ. He started serving others

146

instead of just thinking of himself. His life was so transformed that even his family saw he was a new man in Christ. This former criminal now found it an honor to have the privilege of serving others in the name of Jesus.

Allow faith to spring forth from your life!

"When people take the message home to listen to it over and over and over again, they are given a greater revelation of what's being preached in church... Faith builds up in them, because they're hearing the word of God more and more," says Pastor Josh Payne.

Keep listening until you don't get anything new from the message!

Pastor Schults in the Southeast shares that there are people in his congregation who listen to the message 5, 6, and even 7 times! There is a woman in a sister church who has a large plastic tote of recorded messages in the front seat of her vehicle. She listens to them all the time, passes them out, and tells everyone, "You need to hear this message!"

Application

In nature, living things grow. Growth is a part of life. It is important to develop spiritual growth habits in order to maintain continual spiritual growth and development. Listening to the sermon again during the week and focusing on applying the sermon to your life can be an important growth habit. This habit can help you grow personally while also helping you to be more effective in outreach.

Daily Journal

Describe the habits for spiritual growth that you have already developed. What new spiritual growth habits can you work on developing in your life?

_____

_____

_____

_____

What opportunities have you had recently to share your faith?

_____

_____

_____

_____

Please write your prayer for today. Ask the Lord to help to grow in your spiritual life and to develop habits that help you grow.

_____

_____

_____

_____

Day #36 – EVERYWHERE, EVERYWHERE Share the Gospel

Wherever you are and wherever you go, you may have opportunities to share the Gospel. Too often, it is easy to miss opportunities to share the Gospel. With just a little more preparation and a little more courage, you won't have to miss these opportunities.

As you focus on developing a lifestyle of fruitfulness, you will find yourself sharing the Gospel in many places and with many people that you never imagined. Jesus' heart was moved with compassion as he saw those who came across his path. When you see lives transformed and touched for eternity, your excitement for sharing the Gospel will grow. Ask God to give you his heart for the lost wherever you go.

Power Thought for Today

Paul talks about how he became all things to all men in order that he might win some (I Corinthians 9:22). As you go to different places you will meet people who are different than yourself. You can prepare yourself with messages for people in specific life situations. Seek the Lord for how you might become all things to all men. Ask the Lord to help you to prepare to meet those you will encounter in life with timely and fitting messages.

"I have become all things to all men so that by all possible means I might save some. I do all this for the sake of the Gospel, that I may share in its blessings." – I Corinthians 9:22b-23

Road Trips! Truck drivers! Messages go everywhere he goes!
Although not everyone has the gift of evangelism, anyone can spread the Gospel using CDs and recorded messages. Jerry is a truck driver. He records his own "tracks on audio," and leaves copies in restaurants, truck stops – wherever he goes. A young man just released from prison picked up one of those messages. He listened to it and contacted Jerry's church asking to know more. Jerry has sent him other messages and believes that the man will soon commit his life to Christ. Jerry also found out that this man can't read! A book or tract simply wouldn't have worked – it took an audio message to reach this man with the message of God's love!

$12,000 given to fund the message ministry!

An elderly woman suggested that a man in the community would like a recorded sermon. A man who has a message ministry distributing CDs and tapes gave the man a recorded sermon. The man receiving the message listened to it and sent it to a lady in Michigan. The lady wrote back and asked how much the recordings cost. The man with the message ministry sent her a box of messages and told the lady in Michigan that he was glad that God had made it possible for him to provide the messages free of charge. This lady was put on the mailing list. Within a week or two the gentleman that had started receiving the first message started sending $50 a month to help fund the message ministry. The lady in Michigan started sending $150 per month.

After this happened, the man with the message ministry wanted more duplicators so he could duplicate more than 30 messages at a time. His ministry was growing! The man prayed about this and did not tell anyone about this vision for growth. One day his wife called him. She told him that they had received a check for $12,000 dollars from the lady in Michigan. The man asked his wife if she thought it would be good if the money was used to purchase duplication equipment! His wife thought it was a great idea too. Just imagine how much they could buy with $12,000! God had supplied more than enough for this man's needs and vision! He was able to invest more money than he could have imagined in this ministry.

Messages go everywhere!

A young man and a friend of his were in a laundry facility in North Carolina. His friend encouraged the young man to pick up some messages from a basket in the laundry facility. The young man walked over and picked up some messages. The young man told his friend that he had just been given the two messages from the same minister just days earlier – while he was in California.

An unusual way to give out messages…

One lady has found a unique place to give out messages – drive-through windows! Then, one day her pastor preached a message on "Finding God in a Fast Food Nation." After this message, she got even more excited about sharing the Gospel at drive-through windows. Now, she keeps several copies of the "Finding God in a Fast Food Nation" message in her car.

Shortly after the "Fast Food" message was preached, she went on a trip with another lady. The other lady wondered how her friend gave out messages at drive-through windows! Then, she discovered how easy it was to give out messages at the drive-through. When her friend picked up her food at the drive-through window, she simply said that she had a gift for the person. The person handed her the food, and she handed them a message – spiritual food that could change their life for eternity. "I may never see any of those people again, but I'm praying that God will speak to them through those CDs." What a creative way to share messages! ౿ᗡ

Application

Pray that the Lord gives you opportunities wherever you go to share the Gospel. Think through unique ways and places to share the Gospel. For instance, if you go on vacation with family or friends, you can turn it into an outreach vacation. Just include a bunch of messages in your luggage when you pack and make it a family event to hand out CDs at restaurants and other places you visit.

Or, you can share the Gospel with the people you meet during daily life. Ask the Lord to open your eyes to the opportunities around you to share the Gospel.

Daily Journal

Where are some new places that you can share the Gospel? How can you prepare to share the Gospel in these places?

_____

_____

_____

_____

What opportunities have you had recently to share your faith?

_____

_____

_____

Please write your prayer for today. Ask the Lord to give you courage and creative ideas in sharing the Gospel as you go through daily life.

_____

_____

_____

_____

Day #37 – POWER DAY – God Stories and Personal Testimonies

Power Days: On power days, you will learn how to extend and multiply your impact. Power Days will show you how to increase your outreach impact in your community, how you can help your church multiply its effectiveness, or how to multiply your own personal outreach efforts.

Believers often overlook one of the most powerful tools in reaching others for Christ. As a believer, you are to be witnesses to the things you have seen and heard. You can share with others what God has done in our own life and in the lives of those you know.

Your personal testimony is one of the most powerful things you can share with those who do not know Christ. And, you do not need to have a super dramatic conversion experience to touch the lives of others. You just need an active relationship with Christ. You might share how you found Christ, how the Lord has worked in your life, or how God helped you through a difficult time. Personal testimonies can touch people's hearts in very deep ways. Many people are recording their own personal testimony so that they can share their testimony (or a group of testimonies) with others on DVDs and CDs.

Power Thought for Today

You may not have really thought about your own testimony or God Story as having power, but it is does. As you share your faith with others, you are a witness to the things that you have heard and seen the Lord do in your own life and in the lives of others. Your testimony can have a powerful impact on those around you.

"He (Jesus) said to them: 'It is not for you to know the times or dates the Father has set by his own authority. But you will receive power when the Holy Spirit comes on you; and <u>you will be my witnesses</u> in Jerusalem, and in all Judea and Samaria, and to the ends of the earth.' After he said this, he was taken up before their very eyes, and a cloud hid him from their sight." – Acts 1:7-9 (NIV, emphasis added)

"Therefore, since <u>we are surrounded by such a great cloud of witnesses</u>, let us throw off everything that hinders and the sin that so easily entangles, and let us run with perseverance the race marked out for us." – Hebrews 12:1 (NIV, emphasis added)

Testimonies help church gain five families in two months! Door-to-door ministry...

Several people at a church in Arizona go out into their community each week. They go to different homes and give people messages. They keep it simple, old-fashioned, and effective. They knock on doors and say, "We're giving out a free gift from Shepherd's Church. It contains Christian testimonies." They don't try to get into conversation; they just give people the gifts. Their church has gained five families in two months due to their message ministry.

"One young woman who received a (recorded message) called my wife, weeping and saying she wanted to find God," began Pastor Bryan Showvaker. "She came over to our house and my wife ministered to her. Her father also called and we met with him. He was weeping and saying God had sent us out there just for him and his family. His two sons, daughter, and their families all came back to the Lord. He must have thanked me fifty times in a few days."

"This is how we preach Christ: warning every man and teaching every man all wisdom, that we may present every man perfect in Christ Jesus," Pastor Bryan shared. "The Lord showed me that getting a message into someone's hand is a form of preaching the Gospel."

Man records testimony and sees hundreds come to Christ...

My father, Johnny Berguson, recorded a 16-tape horse training series a number of years ago. My father used biblical principles for child rearing to train horses. With the horse training series, people use the series to learn how to train their own horse. The very last message in the series is called, "The Greatest Horse Training Secret I've Ever Learned." This last message contains my father's Christian testimony and a call for people to make Jesus the Lord of their life.

After buying the horse training course and listening to the last message, many people started getting saved. For years, my father had several people write to him each month to let him know that they had committed their life to Christ, after listening to the last message in the series. He first recorded this training series over 15 years ago, and he continues to hear from people to this day! This message has helped hundreds, perhaps even thousands to find Christ. My father's story demonstrates the creative use of a personal testimony message.

Application

You may be able to record your own testimony or God Story. Or, you may be able to help your church to create a collection of testimonies. Once you have a testimony or a God Story message, this may become one of your favorite messages to give away.

Daily Journal

Today's Date_____

What are some powerful things that God has done in your own life (or the lives of those you know)?

_____

_____

_____

_____

What opportunities have you had recently to share your faith?

_____

_____

_____

_____

Please write your prayer for today. Ask the Lord to give you wisdom in whether you should record your own testimony or God Story. Or, perhaps, you should consider helping your church to create a collection of testimonies or God Stories. Pray and ask God for creative outreach strategies.

_____

_____

_____

_____

Day #38 – Incorporating outreach in your job, your lifestyle

Over the past six weeks, you have heard story after story about regular, ordinary believers who are having an extraordinary impact for God's kingdom. Have you started reaching out and having an impact on the lives of others? The Lord may want you to have this same type of impact that you have been reading about both in your community and beyond.

God may want you to have an impact in your local community, across the nation, or even countries you may never visit. The truth is, you may not even know the full impact that you are being used in advancing God's kingdom as messages begin to spread to regions outside your local community. Perhaps, you will even meet people in heaven that you impacted for eternity but never met while on earth!

Your impact in sharing your faith can continue to grow. You have been praying for God to help activate you in sharing your faith as a lifestyle. Sharing your faith as a lifestyle means that you share your faith wherever life takes you – whether that is to a job, a community activity, or even running errands. God can use you to advance His kingdom anywhere. The Lord can use you in regular daily life to have a remarkable impact for His kingdom.

Power Thought for Today

The Lord has blessed your life through the Gospel. How well are you doing in sharing this good news that has blessed your own life with others? Begin to think of more places and strategies to share the good news of the Gospel with others. Ask the Lord to help your outreach to flourish. Do not withhold good from others – tell others about the good news the Lord has used to bless your life!

"Anyone, then, who knows the good he ought to do and doesn't do it, sins." — James 4:17 (NIV)

Using messages through your job… Your life activities…

Lowell knew he needed help. It became undeniable when his employer told him, "Lowell, your problems are bigger than all your friends and relatives can help you with." Lowell ended up spending four months in a rehab center. Unfortunately, Lowell was no better off on the inside after rehab. But, he went back to work. He ended up attending a motivational seminar. The message was not spiritual, but the speakers gave credit to God for their success. He picked up a message by one of the speakers and tossed it into a drawer...

Lowell tried to make changes in his life over the course of the next year. About a year later, he happened to pull that message back out of the drawer and listened to it. When he pulled the message out of the drawer, he was drawn to it. The message turned out to be about the speaker's spiritual journey, some of the things the speaker had gone through, and how God moved in the speaker's life in a positive way. Listening to the message gave Lowell encouragement.

About a week later, he listened to the message again. He did that for about six months. He kept listening to that same message over and over again. Then, one night he was ready to make a commitment to Christ. He thanked the Lord for dying on the cross for him and asked God to forgive him for all the evil things he had done. He knew he could not only be forgiven but could forgive himself.

At that moment, all the cravings for drugs and alcohol were erased.

Messages help an entire family find Christ!

A lady in Virginia was sent messages of Pastor Robins each week. One day this lady had a yard sale and put the messages in a basket. She put the messages out at the yard sale for people to take. A guy came along and wanted to buy the entire basket of messages. She agreed, and the man took the entire basket of messages. He started listening to the messages as he was traveling to and from work.

Eventually, the man took a trip to visit his sister. It just so happened that the man's sister lived less than 30 miles from Pastor Robin's church. The man talked his sister and her husband into visiting Pastor Robin's church. The man who had taken his sister and her husband to church called the pastor in tears. Both the sister and her husband wanted prayer. They started attending church and gave their lives to Christ. Since then, their children have also found faith in Christ as well! Just one basket of messages helped lead an entire family to Christ!

Application

Continue to press in through prayer and ask the Lord to help you make outreach and fruitfulness a lifestyle. Look for ways to incorporate outreach into your lifestyle whether it be at your job, your community activities, or in just regular daily life. Pray that God would give you boldness. As you step out in faith, ask the Lord to move in power in the hearts and lives of those you meet.

to church and shared that she made a commitment to Christ after listening to the message.

These stories are just the beginning of the impact at this church as they continue to faithfully share the Gospel.

Application

Just like the heroes of the faith from the Scriptures, you can develop a lifestyle of praying and doing what God wants you to do. The Lord is the same yesterday, today, and forever. You can pray daily for the Lord to bring people across your path who need to hear the Gospel and that the Lord would give you wisdom in sharing the Gospel with them.

Today's Date_____

How can you incorporate the concept of 'pray and act' into your life as a habit?

_____

_____

_____

_____

What opportunities have you had recently to share your faith?

_____

_____

_____

Please write your prayer for today. Ask God to help you in hearing His voice and discerning His will. Do what you believe God wants you to do in sharing your faith. Pray and act!

_____

_____

_____

_____

_____

Day #40 – A LOOK AHEAD…

ver the past 40 days, you have heard how God how has used people from all walks of life to touch the lives of others for eternity. As you move beyond these 40 days of outreach, choose to make outreach a lifestyle. Do not let a day go by without praying for opportunities to reach out to others with the love of Christ. Be open to the opportunities that the Lord brings your way to touch lives for eternity. And, be willing to be inspired by the Lord to try creative ideas.

You'll want to continue building a growing collection of outreach messages. Use sermons, special messages, and testimonies.

Power Thought for Today

You may be stepping into one of the most exciting journeys in your entire life… a journey into greater fruitfulness! There is a longing within each of our hearts to experience more fruit for God's kingdom. In order to continue to grow in fruitfulness, you must step out in faith and continue to get closer and closer to Jesus each day.

And remember, you can be ordinary, but you can still be used by God in extraordinary ways. God takes the ordinary and does extraordinary things!

"Salvation is found in no one else, for there is no other name under heaven given to men by which we must be saved. When they saw the courage of Peter and John and realized that they were unschooled, ordinary men, they were astonished and they took note that these men had been with Jesus." – Acts 4:12-13 (NIV, emphasis added)

> *When they saw the courage of Peter and John and realized that they were unschooled, ordinary men, they were astonished...*

An elderly man gets saved after listening to a CD!

There was an elderly man in Florida who had never been saved. He picked up a free CD at a local business and listened to it in his truck as he drove. As he listened to the message, he says that he just felt something. God was moving in his heart. He pulled over his pickup to the side of Highway 19, got out, got on his knees in the grass, and asked Jesus to come into his life to be his Lord and Savior.

A State Trooper saw him kneeling beside the road and got suspicious. By the time the trooper turned his car around, the elderly gentleman was back in his truck and headed down the road. The trooper pulled him over and asked, "Sir, have you been drinking?" "Yes, sir," the man replied, "I've been drinking chocolate milk and the Holy Ghost. I just got saved back there in that grass." The Lord used this message to impact this elderly man's life for eternity.

A message left in a phone booth leads to repentance!

A man by the name of Ron Perkins found a recorded message in a phone booth. The title of the message sparked his curiosity. He took the message home and listened to it. Ron was so moved by the message that he repented of sins and started attending church. His wife also started attending church due to Ron's inspiration. Ron has now been serving the Lord for three years! This all came about from one little message that Ron found in a phone booth. When God uses a message, He can use a message anywhere!

After receiving three messages, Matt came to church and surrendered all to Jesus!

Matt was a young man who was given copies of a pastor's sermons three different times. Each time he was given a copy he was also given an invitation to visit the church. It took three messages before he would even consider going to church. The third time he finally decided to "check it out." He came to church, got saved, and his whole life changed. As he completely surrendered his life to Jesus, it became clear to him that he was called to preach the Gospel. Matt now lives in Alabama and preaches at youth conferences and juvenile detention centers. A man is born again and many more are reached because someone cared enough to give this young man not one, but three messages!

Application

Reaching out to others will require persistence and a willingness to be led by the Holy Spirit. Some people may be touched quickly, while others may take more time. Ask the Lord to give you a heart for those who need Christ and to activate you into a true lifestyle of fruitfulness. It is time to step into a lifestyle of fruitfulness!

Daily Journal

If you were living a total lifestyle of fruitfulness, what would this look like in your life? How often would you share your faith and with whom? Be specific.

_____

_____

_____

What opportunities have you had recently to share your faith?

_____

_____

Please write your prayer for today. Ask God to activate you into the lifestyle of fruitfulness that you have described above. And, pray and ask the Lord to make your heart feel about the lost and their salvation like Christ feels about the lost and their salvation.

_____

_____

Now that you have read this book... what is your personal dream for fruitfulness in your life? What is your vision for reaching out to others? Record your dream for fruitfulness here...

_____

_____

_____

Beyond Day #40... A Challenge...

Throughout the past 40 days, you have heard about countless ordinary people who have had an extraordinary impact for God's kingdom. The last 40 days may just be the beginning of your journey into a lifetime of fruitfulness.

You probably have Christian friends or family members whose lives have not yet been activated into a lifestyle of fruitfulness. If this book has blessed your life, you can pass along this blessing to others. Who in your church, your family, or your community could be activated into a life a greater fruitfulness? Or, who could you share the principles with that you have learned from this book?

Let's see something happen!!!

You have had many opportunities to take the journey into a lifestyle of fruitfulness over the past 40 days. Just imagine if Christians all over your community began to commit to living lifestyles of fruitfulness and started applying proactive principles, prayer, and deliberate action. What would happen in your community?

> *Just imagine if Christians all over your community began to commit to living lifestyles of fruitfulness and started applying proactive principles, prayer, and deliberate action.*

Recently, I was talking to a lady who is pondering the claims of Christ. This lady has had many opportunities to hear the Gospel and learn about the Bible over the past several months. From this period of safe exploration, her heart has changed dramatically. Seeing all the opportunities she has had to learn about the Bible and talk about the Gospel has caused me to desire that all my friends and relatives would have such an in-depth opportunity to consider the claims of Christ. Just imagine... each person you meet is someone's relative, friend, coworker, son, or daughter. Each person you meet is immensely valued by both others and by God.

> *Just imagine... each person you meet is someone's relative, friend, coworker, son, or daughter.*

Here's the challenge...

Do you know of other Christians in your church or community who could be activated into a lifestyle of fruitfulness? Or, perhaps, you have Christian friends or family members who could be activated? If you get activated into a lifestyle of fruitfulness and then you pass this on to others who pass this on to others... you could be part of a grassroots movement in taking the Gospel to our nation and beyond. 🐌

> *If you get activated into a lifestyle of fruitfulness and then you pass this on to others who pass this on to others... you could be part of a grassroots movement in taking the Gospel to our nation and beyond.*

Application

You may be stepping into a lifestyle of fruitfulness greater than you have ever imagined. Now, it is time to think of other Christians who can join you in this journey into greater fruitfulness. There are people you might be able to connect with to reach others for Christ, and there are people who you might be able to help activate into a lifestyle of fruitfulness.

Daily Journal

List the names of Christians who you might be able to help activate into a lifestyle of greater fruitfulness...

_____

_____

_____

_____

_____

_____

What can you do to help activate these Christians? Are there any of these Christians that would benefit from reading a copy of this book?

_____

_____

_____

_____

Note: Because I want to help you activate those you know into a lifestyle of fruitfulness, there is a special discount for ordering multiple copies of this book at www.40DaysToFruitfulness.com. If you sense the Lord leading you to get someone a copy of this book, then do it. My passion in writing this book is to see ordinary Christians activated into a lifestyle of fruitfulness. It is my prayer that more and more Christians are activated into a lifestyle of fruitfulness! And, you can help others get activated into a lifestyle of fruitfulness too!

For Pastors Only

hat would it look like if your entire congregation shared their faith regularly? Churches are seeing 30%, 50%, and even up to 80% of their congregation sharing their faith with those who need to hear the Gospel as they apply the principles described in this book.

If you are a pastor, you went into ministry in order to see lives touched both in the present and for eternity. As your congregation becomes activated in sharing their faith, you will see deeper spiritual growth in your congregation and new lives touched for eternity.

A great way to use this book is as a tool in activating your entire church in outreach. Many churches are using this book as a tool. Your entire congregation can go through the book together as a church. Just set five minutes aside each Sunday for someone to share either about the book or how the Lord is activating them personally in sharing the Gospel. Or, small groups can go through this book as a small group.

> *Just set five minutes aside each Sunday for someone to share either about the book or how the Lord is activating them personally in sharing the Gospel.*

Ask God for wisdom in how you can most effectively use this book as a tool in your church.

One of the most faith-building activities that the people in your church can do is to share their faith with others. Something special happens as people begin to share their faith in Christ with others. Desire for spiritual disciplines such as Bible reading, fellowship, financial giving, and even prayer seem to increase naturally. As your congregation sees the Lord touch the lives of those around them, enthusiasm grows.

Life-giving churches are fun to lead and fun to be a part of. This book provides insight into the tools and strategies that are helping even shy people to share their faith. Just imagine if your entire church, even shy people, were equipped to share the Gospel!

For helpful tools in activating your church in fruitfulness and outreach, see the *Five Free Downloads and Other Tools* page. There are five video downloads available as free downloads that you can show your congregation to help you and your congregation in your journey into greater fruitfulness. These video clips are less than 5 minutes each and can be played during your worship service to help activate your congregation into outreach.

> *Churches are seeing 30%, 50%, and even up to 80% of their congregation sharing their faith as they apply the principles in this book.*

Strategies to implement this book...

Here are simple strategies to use this book as a tool in activating your entire congregation in outreach:

1 – Launch a church-wide initiative. Go through the *40 Days to Fruitfulness* book as a church-wide initiative. Set a goal for what percentage of your congregation you would like to see go through this book. Your church can order copies of this book in bulk. You can also activate your small groups to discuss the book.

2 – Make the initiative visible. Use posters, tracking thermometers, and bulletin inserts to make the initiative visible.

3 – Set aside 5-minutes each Sunday to talk about the journey to fruitfulness. Someone can share a story from the book or how the Lord is activating them personally in sharing their faith. Or, your church can show video clips. Five free video clip downloads are available at www.40DaysToFruitfulness.com that your church can use.

4 – Model outreach. The senior pastor should model outreach. During the sermon, the pastor can share stories of how the pastor is seeking to apply the principles of fruitfulness.

5 – Sign-up for helpful tools, tips, and encouragement for pre-launching the initiative and during the 40 days to fruitfulness.

6 – Get your congregation signed up for short, daily training and motivational segments to accompany the initiative.

7 – Pray, pray, pray. Your church can mobilize prayer teams and your congregation to pray for this initiative.

Extra tools are available at www.40DaysToFruitfulness.com.

Combine the *40 Days to Fruitfulness* with the *Visitor Retention Program* for multiplied impact...

The *40 Days to Fruitfulness* will increase the flow of visitors to your church. Combine this approach with the biblical strategies that will help your church retain more visitors and you'll see a multiplied impact. See the *Visitor Retention Program* on page ____.

Pastor's Journal

How can you use the book *40 Days to Fruitfulness* to activate your congregation into outreach?

_____

_____

_____

_____

It is important for the pastor to model outreach. Are you personally activated in sharing your faith as a lifestyle? What is your vision for fruitfulness in your own life?

_____

_____

_____

_____

Please write your prayer for activating your congregation into outreach. Ask God to help you in activating your congregation to have greater fruitfulness for His kingdom. Do what you believe God wants you to do in activating your congregation.

_____

_____

_____

_____

Five Free Downloads and Other Tools

There are helpful tools available for maximizing the impact of this book. These tools include:
- A daily audio encouragement available as a podcast or delivered to your phone or cell phone.
- Special topic outreach messages.
- Downloads that make it easy and inexpensive to setup your own personal outreach website.
- Tools and tips to help you be more effective in outreach.
- And more.

Church Tools

Tools to help entire churches conduct a *40 Days to Fruitfulness* initiative including:
- Five free video downloads. These downloads are less than 5-minutes each and can be shown during the weekly worship services to help train and inspire the congregation in sharing their faith.
- Tools to make the 40-Day initiative visible including posters, tracking thermometers, and bulletin inserts.
- Advice and tips on how to successfully conduct a *40 Days To Fruitfulness* initiative at your church.
- And more.

Go to www.40DaysToFruitfulness.com.

Because visitors will be coming to your church... here's how to make them stick!

As you apply the principles in this book, your church will see an increase in the number of visitors. This means that it will be more important than ever to retain them!

Discover Kingdom's Retention Program! Kingdom has worked with well over 100,000 churches. There are reasons why some churches grow and others don't. Kingdom wants to share those strategies with you.

Church grows from 280 to 400 people in less than 3 months!

"The Visitor Retention Program has really helped us to focus on making others feel welcome in our church. Before we started, we were right at 280 people assembled and right now we are at 400 – and that's in just 3 months! Our whole church is focused on the Visitor Retention Program. We call it our Five-Star Ministry!"

– Pastor Robert Campbell, NC

Church grows by 30%!

"Early in November we started [the Visitor Retention Program], and Pastors, we have already seen growth! In the 3 short months since we started the program, we went from about 60 people to 80! And we're excited about reaching people for the harvest of God!"

– Pastor Wendell Smith, FL

The principles you will learn have helped other churches retain more than 50% of their first-time visitors! It is important to increase both the number of visitors and the retention of first-time visitors.

Call Kingdom today to get your FREE information over the phone! Soon you'll be on your way to having a more vital and vibrant connection with your visitors – and your church will grow! If you are a layperson, you may even want to sponsor this program for your church.

Kingdom

1-800-788-1122